Politics: A Very Short Introduction

'Kenneth Minogue's book fills a real need, and is the best work of its kind since the publication of Bernard Crick's *In Defence of Politics*. . . . It is meritorious in two significant ways. First, it casts a wide net. . . . Second, it addresses its subject matter with sophistication . . . the book is beautifully written.'
William Maley, *Policy*

'Kenneth Minogue is a very lively stylist who does not distort difficult ideas.'
Maurice Cranston

'Minogue is an admirable choice for showing us the nuts and bolts of the subject.'
Nicholas Lezard, *Guardian*

VERY SHORT INTRODUCTIONS are for anyone wanting a stimulating and accessible way into a new subject. They are written by experts, and have been translated into more than 45 different languages.

The series began in 1995, and now covers a wide variety of topics in every discipline. The VSI library now contains over 500 volumes—a Very Short Introduction to everything from Psychology and Philosophy of Science to American History and Relativity—and continues to grow in every subject area.

Titles in the series include the following:

Kenneth Minogue

POLITICS

A Very Short Introduction

OXFORD

UNIVERSITY PRESS

Great Clarendon Street, Oxford OX2 6DP

Oxford University Press is a department of the University of Oxford.
It furthers the University's objective of excellence in research, scholarship,
and education by publishing worldwide in

Oxford New York

Auckland Bangkok Buenos Aires Cape Town Chennai
Dar es Salaam Delhi Hong Kong Istanbul Karachi Kolkata
Kuala Lumpur Madrid Melbourne Mexico City Mumbai Nairobi
São Paulo Shanghai Taipei Tokyo Toronto

Oxford is a registered trade mark of Oxford University Press
in the UK and in certain other countries

Published in the United States
by Oxford University Press Inc., New York

British Library Cataloguing in Publication Data
Data available

Library of Congress Cataloging in Publication Data
Data available
ISBN 978-0-19-285388-2

Impression: 31

Typeset by RefineCatch Ltd, Bungay, Suffolk
Printed and bound by CPI Group (UK) Ltd, Croydon, CR0 4YY

Foreword

'In our time', Thomas Mann remarked, 'the destiny of man presents its meaning in political terms.' This is certainly true for a lot of bores in universities who believe that one cannot enjoy a poem or conduct a love affair without at the same time making a political statement. At a common-sense level, this view is no less foolish than the sub-Freudian opinion that everything we do is a sexual revelation. As Yeats responded to Mann:

> How can I, that girl standing there
> My attention fix
> On Roman or on Russian
> Or on Spanish politics?

Common sense is the point. In politics things are real and propositions are (more or less) true or false. People bleed and die. Politics, with difficulty, sustains the common world in which we may talk to each other, and philosophers who dissolve experience into perspectives, horizons, sensa, values, dominations, cultures, and the rest will destroy that common world. Politics is the activity by which the framework of human life is sustained; it is not life itself. The sceptical philosopher, the moral relativist, the rancorous academic social critic, the religious visionary, and the artistic seer have their place in our civilization, but their intrusion into politics has not been happy, especially during the last two centuries. Experience shows that politics, for all its capacity to order many ways of life, needs to keep its distance from these adventures. Yet the activity of politics is human life at a stretch, full of heroism and duplicity. To understand it is to know how varied it can be, at this time and that place.

This introduction seeks in a short compass to place politics in both a disciplinary and a historical context. It attempts to bring both the theory and the practice of the activity into a common focus, and along the way to slough off an error or two. But the author fully realizes that one man's error is likely to be another's enthusiastic commitment.

K.M.

September 1994

Contents

Chapter 1

Why Despots Don't Belong in Politics

The story is told of how Harun Al Raschid, the caliph of Baghdad, would disguise himself as a beggar in order to discover what his subjects were thinking. Surrounded by the flatterers who cluster round absolute power, he could discover the truth of things only in devious ways. Harun was the caliph reputed to have condemned Scheherazade to death, who so charmed him with her stories from evening to evening for a thousand nights that he delayed her execution and eventually married her. This story is a famous image of despotism, a system of order created by conquest, resting on fear, and issuing in caprice.

In a despotic system of government, the ultimate principle of order issues from the inclinations of the despot himself. Yet despotism is not a system in which justice is entirely meaningless: it has generally prevailed in highly traditional societies where custom is king and the prevailing terms of justice are accepted as part of the natural order of things. Each person fits into a divinely recognized scheme. Dynasties rise and fall according to what the Chinese used to call 'the mandate of heaven', but life for the peasant changes little. Everything depends on the wisdom of the ruler. In the eleventh century BC the Israelites, having trouble with the Philistines, went to the prophet Samuel who ruled them and asked to have a king who would both judge them and lead them in battle. Samuel warned against this move, advising that such a king would seize their property and enslave their energies. But they insisted that they wanted to be like other nations, and a king they must have. 'King' in this Middle Eastern context meant a ruler who would deal despotically with them, a governor quite different from the constitutional rulers of Europe. As it happened, the Israelites were fortunate to have in Saul, David, and Solomon a line of notable rulers who gave Israel a short taste of order, and even some international glory. Solomon's solution to the problem of two women both claiming the same baby is but the most famous example of his legendary wisdom. But even these monarchs proved oppressive, and in the end the burden of paying for Solomon's grand schemes split Israel apart.

'Despotism' is a catch-all category containing large variations. In one form or another, non-European civilizations have almost invariably been ruled despotically. The Western imagination, however, has generally been repelled by despots – cruel pharaohs, deranged Roman emperors like Caligula and Nero, exotic and remote emperors in India or China. In Europe, the desire for despotic power must disguise itself. Europeans have sometimes been beguiled by a despotism that comes concealed in the seductive form of an ideal – as it did in the cases of Hitler and Stalin. This fact may remind us that the possibility of despotism is remote neither in space nor in time. Many countries are still ruled in this manner, and it can threaten pain or death at any moment; it is like living in a madhouse.

Today we define despotism (along with dictatorship and totalitarianism) as a form of government. This would have horrified the classical Greeks, whose very identity (and sense of superiority to other peoples) was based on distinguishing themselves from the despotism endured by their eastern neighbours. What this contrast reveals is that politics is so central to our civilization that its meaning changes with every change of culture and circumstance. For this reason, our first move in trying to understand politics must be to free ourselves from the unreflective beliefs of the present. One aim of this book is to explain how it came about that what used to be a limited activity conducted by the élites of some Western countries is now thought to be the inescapable preoccupation of mankind.

We need to look first at the value the classical Greeks attached to politics. What the Greeks knew above all was that they were not orientals. They often admired the magnificent cultures of eastern empires such as Egypt or Persia, but usually disdained the way in which they were ruled. They called this foreign system 'despotism' because it seemed no different from the relation between a master and his slaves. As warriors, the Greeks despised the practice by which subjects coming into the presence of an oriental ruler prostrated themselves: they found this an intolerable form of inequality between citizens and their rulers. Over two thousand years later, we inherit precisely the same reflex rejection of prostration, partly because the language of prostration has become the image by which Christianity recognizes the distance between the human and the divine. When we discuss these matters, we often use the Latin term 'domination'. The Greek *despotes* and the Roman *dominus* both signify the specific form of power exercised by the master of slaves. The modern use of 'dictatorship' and the twentieth-century coinage of 'totalitarianism' are among the many recent signs of the undiminished centrality of this idea in our self-understanding.

The essence of despotism is that there is no appeal, either in practice or in law, against the unchecked power of the master. The sole object of the subjects must be to please. There is no parliament, no opposition, no free press, no independent judiciary, no private property protected by law from the rapacity of power, in a word, no public voice except that of the despot. Such powerlessness is, oddly enough, the reason why despotisms are notable generators of spiritual enlightenment. A reaction sets in against a world governed by the caprice of power, and thoughtful subjects take up mysticism, Stoicism, and other forms of withdrawal. The essence of life is then found in a spiritual realm beyond that of the senses, and social and political life is devalued as illusion. The

3

result is usually scientific and technological stagnation except in the short term.

Despotism flows so naturally from the military conquest in which most societies originate that creating a civil or political order must be recognized as a remarkable achievement. Europeans have managed it on three notable occasions, and on two of them the achievement collapsed. The first was in the city-states of classical Greece, which sank into despotism after the death of Alexander the Great. The second was among the Romans, whose very success created an empire so heterogeneous that only a despotic power could prevent it from falling apart. The first of these experiences generated Stoicism and other philosophies of withdrawal from the world, and the second was the seed-bed of Christianity. From Christianity and the barbarian kingdoms of the west emerged the medieval version of politics from which in turn evolved the politics of our modern world. Since we live within this experience, we can only catch it on the wing, as it were, and we do not yet know what its final destiny will be.

We do know, however, that the rejection of despotism on which the Western tradition has largely rested is now ambivalent. Many in recent centuries have dreamed of using the irresistible power only found in despotism for removing the evident imperfections of our world. The project of despotism in Europe, even of a philosophical or enlightened kind, would fail unless its real character were concealed. Since politics is in part a theatre of illusion, new names and concepts are easy to invent, and in the twentieth century totalitarian versions of the dream of despotism constructed a vast political laboratory in which different versions of the project of creating a perfect society were put to the test. That they failed is currently recognized by all; it is less widely recognized that such immense convulsions must correspond to profound tendencies in our civilization. To understand politics must therefore include studying the signs which might tell us what is going on beneath the surface of this and other fault-lines in our civilization.

4

One widely recognized clue is the current state of the distinction between private life and the public world. The private world is that of the family, and of individual conscience as each individual makes his or her own choice of beliefs and interests. Such a private life would not be possible without the overarching public world of the state, which sustains a structure of law appropriate to a self-determining association. Politics only survives so long as this overarching structure of public law recognizes its own limits. As Pericles put it in his famous funeral oration for Athenians killed in the first year of the Peloponnesian War: 'We are free and tolerant in our private lives; but in public affairs we keep to the law.' The actual boundary, both in law and in people's attitudes, between what is public and what is private is, of course, constantly changing. Homosexuality and religion, which used to be publicly regulated, are now largely private, while rape within marriage and abuse of children are increasingly subject to law. It is the fact of recognizing such a division which distinguishes politics – we may loosely identify it with freedom and democracy – from despotism.

In the classic despotisms everything in society was the private property of the despot, but in the modern world this basic distinction has been steadily eroded from the other side: ever larger areas of private life have come to be publicly regulated. If everything controversial is called 'political', and if (as a popular slogan has it) the personal is the political, then nothing is left outside the scope of control by government. This argument has not been universally accepted, but it has been the basic premiss of twentieth-century totalitarianism, and its effect is clearly to lock the individual within a single system of control, destroying the inheritance of distinct and independent roles (economic, religious, cultural, social, and legal) which modern states have until recently enjoyed.

Slogans such as 'the personal is the political' are proposals for action disguised as truths about the world. The meaning of such slogans is often obscure, but they contain sleeping implications which may awaken in new circumstances and demand policies which affront other cherished values, such as individual freedom. It is said that the price of freedom is vigilance, and an important form of vigilance is attention to political rhetoric, which often reveals how things are going.

The beginning of wisdom in politics is attention to signs of change. As a theatre of illusion, politics does not reveal its meanings to the careless eye. Reality and illusion are central categories of political study. The problem begins with the very names of institutions. The dominance of Western fashions means that every country now has a kind of politics, and a complement of institutions – parliaments, constitutions, schedules of rights, trade unions, courts, newspapers, ministers, and so on – which suggests that the same kind of thing is going on all over the world. Nothing could be further from the truth. Japan, for example, has a figure called a prime minister, and many mistakes have been made by foreign statesmen who are frustrated to discover that the Japanese prime minister cannot deliver national policies in the way that rulers of other countries sometimes can. Again, in 1936, Stalin promulgated what was widely claimed to be the most advanced constitution in the world, awash with rights and safeguards for the people of the Soviet Union. The reality was that Stalin was at that very moment engaged in 'purging' the Soviet élite in faked trials. His subjects were being shot by the million. It is not unknown for politicians to lie, but much more confusing is the complex relation between names and reality.

Above all, the name of politics itself. When concepts are stretched too far, they snap and lose their usefulness. 'Politics' used to refer merely to the actions of monarchs, parliaments, and ministers, and to the activities of the politically committed who helped or hindered their accession to authority. Everything else was social or private life. With the expansion of the power of governments, nearly everything has come to be described, in one way or another, as 'political'. We may mention here just one of the many reasons for this. Governments wishing to claim credit for all good things, and oppositions wishing to dispense blame for all bad things, have colluded in spreading the idea that all things, good and bad, are caused by political policies. This idea can turn subjects into petitioners of government, from which all benefits seem to flow, and that in turn reinforces the idea that everything actually *is* political.

There is another reason why politics has expanded its role and meaning. It has immemorially in Europe been the business of monarchs and their servants, and history has largely been the narrative of their doings. To participate in politics has thus been to attain a kind of immortality. When Fidel Castro first attempted, and failed, to take over Cuba in 1953, he defended himself at his trial in a speech declaring: 'History will absolve me.' He conceived of himself theatrically, an actor on the stage of history. Whoever seeks a kind of immortality in history goes into politics. Potential Cromwells are no longer content to be 'guiltless of their country's blood' and to end in the silence of a country churchyard. They go into politics. The French Revolution brought just such fame to otherwise obscure in-dividuals like Robespierre, Danton, Marat, Charlotte Corday, St Just, and others. Revolutionaries are the graffiti artists of history. These are the extreme cases, and for the most part this passion in its milder forms has been satisfied by giving everyone the vote. Universal suffrage is, of course, a form of inflation which has diminished the value of a vote, but it remains essential to our conception of what it is to be a proper human being. 'Alice makes her mark on history' headlined one British newspaper reporting an elderly Black South African voting for the first time in 1994.

We moderns (and especially those who think of themselves as post-moderns) are peculiarly liable to fall into confusion about the nature of politics: we have invented ingenious reasons for thinking that our ideas are superior to those of our ancestors. All cultures believe that their own ideas are the only right ones, but educated people today are unusually locked into the prejudices of the present moment. The doctrine of progress, for example, suggested to many people that *our* convictions were grander than the obviously defective ideas of the past. Contemporary intellectual fashion does indeed reject the idea of progress, and emphasizes how much we bear the imprint of our place and time; it affirms that one culture is the equal of another. This has the appearance of a form of scepticism liberating us from the arrogance of our ancestors, for it seems to reduce our opinions to the same level as those of everyone else. That appearance is an illusion. Contemporary scepticism is a fake humility, masking a dogmatic conviction that our very openness makes our relativist humanism superior both to the dogmatism of the past and the intolerance of other cultures.

Whoever writes about politics must therefore warn against the dangers of the parochialism of one's own time, and this is certainly no less necessary today than before. This widely recognized danger is the reason that the study of politics has always been at the centre of a liberal education. Greek and Roman aristocrats studied law, philosophy, and the art of public speaking in order to fulfil the political vocation indicated by their birth. Politics could be the core of education because it very quickly became a self-conscious activity which provoked reflection and generated a superb literature. Philosophers like Plato and Aristotle explored its conceptual structure; historians like Herodotus kept alive the story of its development; political scientists (Aristotle for example) studied constitutions and how institutions worked; Aesop turned political wisdom into fable; memorable orators like Demosthenes and Cicero assembled the forms of argument most appropriate to persuading an audience; poets wrote elegies and satires on political themes, and political situations were the events which most fired the imagination of Shakespeare and other dramatists. There is no form of understanding and imagination which has not taken politics for its theme.

Many are the mirrors of politics, whose substance can only be grasped by consolidating these images until they compose a coherent scheme of understanding. The politician's immediacy and the don's detachment alike have much to offer. We must try to incorporate both. What

Machiavelli sought as the 'effective truth' of politics is merely what is relevant to the activist. It leaves much out. We must begin by looking at the very different ideas of those who laid the foundations of our conception of politics: the Greeks and Romans.

Chapter 2
The Classical Greeks: How to be a Citizen

Politics among the ancient Greeks was a new way of thinking, feeling, and above all being related to one's fellows. Citizens varied in wealth, beauty, and intelligence, but as citizens they were equal. This was because citizens were rational, and the only appropriate relation between rational beings is that of persuasion. Persuasion differs from command in assuming equality between speaker and listener. Plato provides a noble vision of this form of political life in his dialogue the *Crito*. The philosopher Socrates, having been sentenced to death for corrupting the youth, refused the offer of help to escape Athens, arguing that to flee would be rationally inconsistent with the commitment to the city expressed in the way he had lived his whole life. Even the mode of his execution reflected this basic belief that violence was not an appropriate relation between citizens: he was given a cup of hemlock to drink. The Greek freely obeyed the law of his *polis* and was proud to do so. His very identity was bound up with his city. The worst of fates was exile, a form of civic death sometimes imposed by the convention of ostracism on Athenian statesmen whose power was thought to threaten the constitution.

Among the Greeks we find most of the conditions of freedom: a life lived among equals, subject only to law, and ruling and being ruled in turn. The Greeks were the first historical people to create societies having this form; certainly they were the first to create a literature exploring it as an experience. Politics was the activity specific to this new thing called a 'citizen'. It might take many forms, even the debased forms of tyranny and usurpation, but on one thing the later classical Greeks were adamant: oriental despotism was not politics.

Such is the formal position, and these were the forms which left so deep an imprint on our civilization. The reality was no doubt a great deal more complex. Democratic and oligarchic factions fought bitter battles within cities. Farmers lived on the edge of destitution, and bad harvests might impel them towards debt slavery. Equality within cities was not matched by equal relations *between* cities, and war was endemic. The Greeks were a talkative, passionate people, and their politics was often violent and sometimes corrupt. None of this qualifies, however, the fact that they were capable of brilliant exploits, such as their victory in repelling (and ultimately conquering) their Persian neighbours. In reading much of the literature of their time, we find it easy to think of them as our contemporaries: being rationalists, they speak across the millenniums to us, their cultural descendants, with a deceptive fluency. For all the common ground, however, they were immensely different from us, in their religion, their customs, and their conception of human life. It is this difference which makes studying their civilization so exhilarating.

The Greeks were humanists, but of a kind strikingly different from the humanism (transformed by Christianity) found in the modern world. Their basic proposition was that man is a rational animal, and that the meaning of human life is found in the exercise of rationality. When men succumbed to the passions, they were shamefully descending to a lower form of being. When pride, or hubris, led them to think they were gods, they lost sight of their human limitations and suffered nemesis, the destructive resentment of the gods. The secret of life was human self-knowledge, and a balanced expression of one's human capacities. In deliberating about law and public policy, man found his highest and purest form of self-expression. It could only be enjoyed in the political life of a city.

Humanists often look to the Greeks as ancestors, but their view of the world has one remarkable (and in modern terms, disturbing) implication. Since some are less rational than others, so also are they less human. Slaves in particular are defective in rationality when compared to masters. Those who explored this view, above all the philosopher Aristotle, were perfectly aware that some slaves are clever and some masters stupid; they were merely expounding what they took to be the rational foundation of the institution itself. Again, women were taken to be less rational than men, though Aristotle considered the barbarians to be quite wrong in thinking that they were indistinguishable from slaves. Citizenship was thus confined to free adult males, and in some cities not even to all of those. The activity of politics and that of waging war merged with each other, and it thus seemed natural that women should live domestic lives: they could hardly stand their ground in a phalanx. It might seem that, in taking this view, the Greeks were the prisoners of the prejudices of their time. Being immensely imaginative in their exploration of the world, however, they had no difficulty imagining women doing any number of things: becoming warriors in the form of Amazons; going on a sexual strike to enforce peace in the *Lysistrata* of Aristophanes; taking the role of philosopher–rulers in the Guardians of Plato's *Republic*; but these images were not the reality of everyday life.

The laws and policies of a Greek city emerged, then, not from the palace of a despot, but from discussion among notionally equal citizens in the *agora*, the market-place which also generally served as the arena of politics. Citizens enjoyed equality before the law (*isonomia*, a term sometimes used as a synonym for democracy) and an equal opportunity to speak in the assembly. In a large city such as Athens, thousands of people might turn up to such meetings, so that the speakers were predominantly aristocrats who had studied the art of speaking, or notable leaders who had managed to acquire a band of supporters. In democracies, many offices were filled by lot, but the main officers were elected and were commonly from powerful families. In Thucidides' history of the Peloponnesian War we can see the democratic process at work – for example in the Athenian debate, reported in Book III, as to how the people of Mitylene, who had rebelled against Athenian hegemony, should be punished. In this debate, the popular leader Cleon put the case for confirming the decision already taken to kill the men and sell the women and children into slavery. Cleon appealed to realism: if you want to have an empire, he argued, then you must be prepared to do the ruthless things necessary to keep it together. His opponent, Diodotus, argued for clemency on the ground that ruthlessness would merely turn every occasion of revolt among the clients of Athens into a life and death struggle. It was Diodotus who triumphed in this vivid intellectual contest.

The citizens who participated in the debates belonged in their private lives to households (*oikia*) which were the basic productive units of this ancient world. The *oikos* (from which our term 'economics' derives) was a system of orderly subordination described by Aristotle: subordination of female to male, of children to parents, and of slaves to masters. The household was the sphere in which the Greeks enjoyed family life and largely supplied their material needs: for food, warmth, shelter, procreation, and so on. Here was the world of nature in which everything had its season. In many civilizations, the distinction between artifice and nature is not developed, but it was the basis of the Greek understanding of the world. The idea that wisdom consisted in following the dictates of nature led to divergent philosophies, according to the way in which the concept of 'nature' developed. Greek political philosophy began in meditation upon the tension between recognizing that the *polis* was in one sense natural and in another sense a thing of artifice.

On becoming an adult, the young Greek male could step out of the household into the *agora*, where he found the freedom to transcend natural necessity and take responsibility, uttering words worth remembering and doing deeds that might give him a kind of immortality. The Greeks of the classical period were self-conscious enough to see themselves as a distinct culture, and it is in creating a historical understanding of themselves and their world that they were opening up quite new possibilities of human experience. Politics and history were thus born together, for they share the same conception of what a human being is, and what is worth remembering.

History was the memory of words and deeds, and words were the vehicles of memory. In political activity, men addressed each other in speech, which is a skill to be learned. It requires the marshalling of ideas, the construction of arguments, the capacity to understand an audience, a recognition of the dominant passions of human nature, and much else. For the first time in history, public decisions were made in the clear light of day and subject to open criticism. The skill of rhetoric was codified by teachers called 'sophists' for the benefit of ambitious young aristocrats whose power depended on swaying a popular audience. A speech was a performance to be remembered down the ages. Thucidides tells the story of the Peloponnesian War largely in terms of the arguments adduced in the speeches of the participants; taken together, these speeches amount to a comprehensive manual on political wisdom and political folly.

This approach to political thought and action was the product of one striking false belief, which remains influential to this day: the idea that everything in the world was the result of deliberate design. The Greeks believed their own cities to have been founded by semi-divine figures, such as Lycurgus in the case of Sparta, and Theseus in the case of Athens. Wise men were sometimes called on to restore some such design if it had fallen into disrepair. In politics, the most famous case of this was that of Solon at Athens in the early part of the sixth century BC.

Two features of Solon's reforms illustrate essential features of Greek politics.

The first is that he was careful to base politics on territorial units which mixed up clan or tribal loyalties. The modern constituency, which lumps together all the heterogeneous people living in a given area, has the same effect of breaking down natural loyalties and encouraging people to act politically in terms of broad interests shared widely throughout a community.

The second is that, after establishing his reforms, Solon was careful to leave Athens for ten years so that the new constitution could be operated by others – an early version of the principle of the separation of powers. For the key to politics in the strict sense is that it is a nexus of abstract offices to which duties are attached, and in principle the work may be done by any competent office-holder. Whereas despotism depends on the personality (and often the caprice) of the individual despot, political rulers act in terms of the duties attaching to their offices.

The set of offices by which a *polis* was governed, and the laws specifying their relation, are the *constitution*. Government without a constitution would lack the specific kind of moral limitation which distinguishes politics. Constitutions function into two essential ways: they circumscribe the power of the office-holders, and as a result they create a predictable (though not rigid and fixed) world in which the citizens may conduct their lives. It is constitutions which give form to politics, and the study of them led to the emergence of political science.

A science of politics (as opposed to despotism) is possible because politics itself follows regular patterns, even though it is ultimately at the mercy of the human nature from which it arises. All that one can confidently say about despotism is that able rulers will sooner or later be followed by mad or feeble heirs. A despotism is thus subject to a fixed rhythm of rise and fall, like the seasons, and this confirmed the Greeks in their belief that despotisms, as associations of slaves, were unfree and belonged to the non-rational sphere of nature. But constitutions, because they belong to the sphere of rationality, can be studied in a more scientific way than despotisms, despite their ultimate fallibility.

For one thing, they can be classified according to certain characteristics which reveal dominant tendencies. In all constitutions, the ruler is either a monarch, or a small group of powerful leaders, or a popular assembly. There are no other possibilities than that rule must be by one, or a few, or by the many. During the classical period of Greek politics, the main division was between oligarchic states, which were thought to favour the rich and powerful, and democracies, which responded to the interests of the poor, and which were commonly thought violent and unstable.

Greek political science studied constitutions and generalized the relation between human nature and political associations. Perhaps its most powerful instrument was the theory of recurrent cycles. Monarchies tend to degenerate into tyranny, tyrannies are overthrown by aristocracies, which degenerate into oligarchies exploiting the population, which are overthrown by democracies, which in turn degenerate into the intolerable instability of mob rule, whereupon some powerful leader establishes himself as a monarch and the cycle begins all over again. This is the version of political science we find influentially expounded by a later Greek called Polybius whose main concern was to explain the character of Roman politics to his fellow Greeks; other versions of a political cycle are to be found in Plato and Aristotle.

Knowledge, as Bacon remarked, is power, and the knowledge of this cyclical rhythm in politics provoked the thought that institutions might be arranged in such a way as to break the cycle, allowing states to achieve, if not immortality, at least some long-term stability. The secret of breaking the cycle of decline lay in two propositions. The first was that government consists of a number of functions which may be parcelled out among different offices and assemblies. Executive decision requires a leader, deliberation about policy requires a small group of experienced citizens, while the acceptability of laws and the responsiveness of government depend upon effective ways of consulting the people. This is an argument for constructing a constitution in which power is distributed between the one, the few, and the many. The second proposition is that the very same distribution may also balance the interests of rich and poor, to prevent either from using political power for the purpose of economic exploitation. Such balance in politics was the equivalent of health in the body, and might keep corruption at bay for a very long time. Such is the theory of the balanced constitution which has played a central part in the politics of the West. It represents as a theory what practical politicians often evolve for themselves. The English constitution, for example, evolved into a balance between monarch, Commons, and Lords and is often cited as an example of this theory. Lawyers and statesmen were, indeed, aware of the theory, and sometimes it helped to guide them, but the actual institutions of British politics responded basically to the specific conditions of life in Britain.

It was Aristotle's view that some element of democracy was essential to the best kind of balanced constitution, which he called a 'polity'. He studied many constitutions, and was particularly interested in the mechanics of political change: revolutions, he thought, always arose out of some demand for equality. Concerning himself with both politics and ethics, he posed one question which has been found especially fascinating: can a good citizen be a good man? Rulers in some states may demand of their subjects actions which are wrong. Greek politics (like everything else in the Greek world) was powerfully theorized, to such an extent that it has often been thought that we rattle around within the limited set of possibilities revealed to us by Greek experience. Political judgement, to put the matter another way, is a choice between finite possibilities. This view assumes that human nature is fixed, and has been challenged, especially in modern times, by the view that human beings are always the creatures of their society. Very few possibilities that we discuss were not recognized in one form or another by the Greeks, who also left behind – indeed, it was their speciality – visions of the ideal: in philosophy, Plato's *Republic*, and in politics, the account of Athens put into the mouth of Pericles by Thucidides in his history of the Peloponnesian War.

Chapter 3
The Romans: The Real Meaning of Patriotism

The politics of Greece was based on reason, that of the Romans on love – love of country, love of Rome itself. The Romans thought of their city as a family, and of its founder Romulus as the ancestor of them all. This was quite different from the Greeks, for whom the family signified at the philosophical level merely those necessities in our animal nature which the freedom of politics transcended. It was the great Christian Saint Augustine who made much of patriotism as the guiding passion of the Romans, partly because he saw in it a prefiguring of the love which animated Christians. *Dulce et decorum est pro patria mori* – 'Sweet and fitting it is to die for one's country' – wrote the Roman poet Horace, in a line which long represented the noblest of political sentiments. But times change, and after the vast casualties of the First World War, this very line was often used ironically to signify the helplessness of individuals caught up in the aggressive schemes of politicians. How this change came about is an important part of our story.

The Greek cities were a dazzling episode in Western history, but Rome had the solidity of a single city which grew until it became an empire, and which out of its own decline created a church that sought to encompass nothing less than the globe itself. Whereas the Greeks were brilliant and innovative theorists, the Romans were sober and cautious farmer-warriors, less likely than their predecessors to be carried away by an idea. We inherit our ideas from the Greeks, but our practices from the Romans, and each has left a different imprint on the various nations of modern Europe. German infatuation with the Greeks, for example, has been notably greater than that of the British and the French, for whom Rome was the great exemplar. All Europeans, however, have benefited from the inheritance of two quite distinct vocabularies with which to explore political life: the political vocabulary of the Greeks – policy, police, politics itself – and the civic vocabulary of the Romans – civility, citizen, civilization. Both the architecture and the terminology of American politics, for example, are notably Roman.

The Roman vocabulary is in fact even more fundamental than the Greek because Latin was the language in which politics was understood not only when Rome ruled the Western world but also for a thousand years afterwards in Europe, until the emergence of the modern state in the sixteenth century. We talk of the fall of the Roman empire, but the collapse of Rome's political power (in the Western empire) went hand in hand with the rise of the spiritual empire of the papacy. Indeed, the peoples of what we call the 'Middle Ages' (from about 400 to about AD 1500) long retained the conviction that they were still living amid the ruins of Rome. Sometimes they even tried to revive it. Charlemagne, king of the Franks, was crowned emperor in Rome in AD 800, and the Holy Roman Empire continued in a shadowy form until it was abolished in 1806 by Napoleon, who was setting his own dynasty up in its place, at the same time littering France with monuments in the Roman style. At the beginning of the modern period, Machiavelli presented Roman politics as a model for Europe in his *Discourses on the First Ten Books of Livy* (1518). There is much to be said for Marx's view that the French Revolution was a charade played out in Roman dress.

The Rome that so bewitched Europeans provided a variety of models to explore. The Italian poet Dante in the late Middle Ages admired the empire which brought peace to the world, while Machiavelli presented the virtue of the early republic for admiration. Both responded to the story of Rome as the endlessly fascinating adventures of a people who thought of themselves as having a mission to *civilize* the world. Founded according to legend in 753 BC by Romulus, Rome was ruled by kings until 509 BC when Tarquin the Proud was expelled by Junius Brutus at the head of an aristocratic faction infuriated (so the story goes) by the rape of Lucretia. As a result, the Romans identified kingship with servitude, but in recasting their constitution, they exhibited their characteristic political creativity by a profound modification of their constitution which yet left most of the scaffolding standing. Even monarchy, which was replaced by two consuls jointly holding the *imperium* of the royal office, retained a vestigial presence in the form of a religious official called the *rex sacrorum*. The Senate, which held the *auspicia* (the symbols and instruments of rule), sustained the continuity of the Roman political tradition. Some place had always been found for the participation of the plebeians, the other main class of Romans, but in a state now ruled by patricians rather than by a king standing above both classes, it turned out to be insufficient. Oppressed, as they thought, by the patricians, the plebeians in a body walked out of Rome and set themselves up on a neighbouring hill. The Romans solved this problem in a typical way: by a *foedus*, or treaty, which allowed the plebeians to have office-holders of their own, called tribunes of the plebeians. The exemplary story of Roman politics consists partly in these constitutional responses to crisis, and partly in the heroic exploits in war which they made possible, as the Romans fought and defeated first their neighbours, then the Greek cities of southern Italy, and above all the Carthaginians against whom they fought three desperate wars before triumphing. Before long they had conquered Greece itself and were ruling the entire Mediterranean coastline, along with western Europe including England and part of Germany.

Roman history revolves around the dramatic events through which the republic gave way to the empire. Julius Caesar was assassinated by Marcus Brutus, Cassius, and their followers in 44 BC, but the assassins were defeated by Caesar's nephew Octavian and his partner, Mark Antony. When these two fell out, Octavian defeated Antony at the battle of Actium in 31 BC and returned to Rome bent on recasting the constitution to fit the new circumstances. He did this with such success that what he ruled as an empire retained the forms of a republic for the next two hundred years.

Rome is the supreme example of politics as an activity conducted by men holding offices which clearly limit the exercise of power. When the Romans thought about power, they used two words in order to acknowledge an important distinction: *potentia* meant physical power, while *potestas* signified the legal right and power inhering in an office; in addition, all offices shared in the *imperium*, or the total quantum of power available to the Roman state.

Both these forms of power however were separate from another idea which constituted the most distinctive contribution of the Romans to politics: *auctoritas*. Significantly, this term represented the junction of politics with the Roman religion, which involved the worship of families, and hence of ancestors. An *auctor* or author was the founder or initiator of something – a city, a family, even a book or an idea. The reservoir of *auctoritas* lay in the Senate as the body closest to the ancestors. It has been characterized as more than advice but less than command, and the Romans' respect for it was the real source of their political skill. It was in no sense a kind of political power, but those charged with the conduct of the *res publica*, or public business did not lightly ignore it.

Rome became fascinating to other peoples as its power expanded, and in the second century BC, when Rome conquered the Hellenic world, the Greek historian Polybius explained to his fellow Greeks what this new hegemon, or master of the world, was like. Skilled in the Greek science of the cyclical degeneration of governments, Polybius explained the success of Rome by the fact that one could not really describe her constitution as monarchical, or aristocratic, or democratic, for it contained elements of all three. The result of this combination of powers, he wrote, 'is a union which is strong enough to withstand all emergencies, so that it is impossible to find a better form of constitution than this'. He admired above all the steadiness with which the Senate responded to the greatest disaster in its history: the defeat at Cannae by Hannibal the Carthaginian, in 218 BC. Hannibal sent to Rome a delegation of captured Romans who were pledged to return to their captors after negotiating the ransom of their fellow prisoners. The Romans refused to ransom their soldiers in spite of the gravity of the situation, but sent the delegation back to Hannibal as honour required.

Rome's fame largely rested on a moral strength evident to all who had dealings with her. Bribery of officials was a capital crime, and Romans could be relied on to stand by their oaths. Polybius felt the need to justify this characteristic to his cynical fellow Greeks: the Romans had, he agreed, adopted superstitious beliefs about punishment in the afterlife, but only because this was the best way of making the people virtuous. The Jews, who encountered the Romans at about the same period, felt a similar admiration for so steady an ally: none of their generals, it was noted, 'made any personal claim to greatness by wearing the crown or donning the purple'. In those earlier days, love of country predominated, but in time success and wealth began to corrupt the Romans, who then fell under the sway of despotic forms of order which they had previously found repugnant. Virtue and freedom declined together. It was the literature of Rome, especially the work of Cicero, that persuaded later Europeans that virtue was the condition of freedom.

Acute as he was, Polybius failed to recognize that most un-Greek feature on which so much of the distinctive character of Roman politics rested: *auctoritas*. This was the moral fluid in which was suspended the Roman conviction that the good of the *patria* must take precedence over merely private concerns (such as saving one's life). This moral was conveyed in many famous stories of Roman heroes. Within this overarching concern for Rome itself, however, Romans were immensely competitive and indeed often quarrelsome. Later writers thought the antipathy between patrician and plebeian which runs through the early history of Rome was a weakness, but Machiavelli, in disagreeing with this judgement, put his finger on one of the central features of the whole Western political tradition. He argued that conflict within the state, so long as it was subordinated to the public interest, merely reflected the Roman concern for liberty and for the protection of civil rights. The policy of Rome, like that of the Greeks, issued not from some supposedly supreme wisdom but from a freely recognized competition between interests and arguments within a society. Western politics is distinguished from other forms of social order by its exploration of this theme: that beyond the harmony that results from everyone knowing his place is another harmony, in which conflict is resolved by the free discussion and free acceptance of whatever outcome emerges from constitutional procedure.

Chapter 4
Christianity and the Rise of the Individual

We have so far taken snapshots of politics among the Greeks and Romans, but we may now exhibit the process of politics coming into existence all over again, and in a new setting. During the Middle Ages, civic order emerged in western Europe out of brutality and violence, and for the first time religion played an independent role. To show this as the massive achievement it actually was is to collide with current prejudice, which commonly takes 'feudal' and 'medieval' to be terms of abuse. But 'feudal' merely signifies a specific form of order emerging out of violence, while 'medieval' is the term educated men of early modern times used to refer to the thousand-year stretch that separated them from the Classical period. There is much to be said for the view that the thousand years between the fall of the Roman empire and the emergence of the modern world is the most important strand of all in the weaving of our political texture.

Europe as we know it is the outcome of successive waves of migration by tribes pushed westwards by the pressure of others behind them. They were attracted by the evident prosperity and civilization of the Roman empire. Travelling in great hordes, the wandering peoples whom we know from the names the Romans gave them – Huns, Goths, Visigoths, Angles, Franks, and so on – pushed into the empire over many centuries, at first being absorbed by the Roman structure but later disrupting and destroying it. These barbarians set up kingdoms of their own in the countryside and in time were converted to Christianity. Each realm had a king and a set of magnates who were generally granted land in return for allegiance. Temporary grants of land soon became hereditary, but it took centuries for the old stability of the Roman era to return, partly because of internal quarrels and partly because of the pressure of new wanderers in search of land and security. The Anglo-Saxons, for example, conquered England only to find themselves attacked by the Danes, and then the Normans. These Normans themselves originated in a set of Viking raiders who in the ninth century had carved out a province in the kingdom of the Franks, and went on to create another empire in Sicily. In these troubled times, the only security came from protection by a class of professional warriors. And protection came at a price.

Civil order thus had to be reinvented, and here we shall consider three of the elements out of which the civilization of the high Middle Ages was constructed. The first was the vital love of freedom inherited from the barbarians themselves. In spite of the actual violence of these ages, the barbarian tribes had a powerful moral and legal sense of themselves as the inheritors of a tribal law on which their very identity was based. These were people whose pride consisted in subjection to those to whom they were bound by oath. Kings were the guardians of law. Violence and disorder resulted from the fact that a strong moral and legal sense of how to treat one's own community was in no way paralleled by any sense of the significance of others. It took the religion of Christianity and the morality of courtly love to begin the diffusion of this particular lesson. Europeans found their very identity in submission to a law which they believed themselves to inherit from their ancestors. Law was, as it were, untouched by human will, and it was to be some centuries before the idea that one might *legislate* began to be entertained. This was an idea which came in time from a renewed familiarity with Roman law.

Politics in these early times was, then, the dealings between a king and his more important vassals. It focused around small, primitive, moving courts. But gradually these kings evolved from being the leaders of tribes to being the masters of realms, and the law of which they were custodians became a law of the land rather than a tribe. In England, the kings steadily extended the scope of 'the king's peace' and made themselves available to the lowest in the land as a court of appeal against the exactions of their own direct vassals. And in all these local processes (the details of which varied across Europe) one fact stood out: civil order had to be constructed by agreement with a set of magnates whose control over their own tenants gave them an independent position of their own. This is the second element crucial in the re-emergence of politics. It has been plausibly suggested that the uniqueness of European feudalism resulted from the fact that Europe is a well-watered continent and that its agriculture, unlike that of China, India, and the Middle East, does not depend upon the construction of large dams and canals for irrigation and flood control. Such enterprises require great central power for the mobilization of labour, and characteristically issue in a despotic form of order. Where the weather better distributes what agriculture requires, local life is relatively independent of central power, and authority must consult with its subjects. Like all grand theories of social causation, this one needs to be treated with caution, but it is certainly part of the truth. That it cannot be the whole truth is clear, for nothing in human society is independent of the ideas people have about their situation, and no idea is generated purely by physical necessity.

The theory does, however, help to explain the political structure which emerged in Europe in the second half of the medieval millennium. By the eleventh century we find a mosaic of principalities ruled by dukes and counts, some independent trading cities, and the beginnings of realms out of which we can, with hindsight, see the nation-states of Europe emerging. To the historian, all things are contingent, and the national order of European states solidified gradually out of whole successions of unpredictable events. The Treaty of Verdun in 843, which divided the realm of Charlemagne into three parts, is often taken to be the watershed which gave us France, Germany, and that third kingdom, never fully unified, which stretches from the Netherlands in the north to Savoy and Lombardy in the south. As another example of contingency, we might take the Provençal state which might have emerged in southern France had not the crusade against the Albigensian heretics in the early thirteenth century devastated that area and subjected it to the French monarchy. Kings intrigued, nobles fought wars, and it was the intermixture of policy and accident that determined which among the variety of languages and cultures in Europe came to be identified with nations. Some fashions, however, spread spontaneously all through Europe. The fashion for courtly romance, for example, seems to have emerged first in Provence and the surrounding regions, but had immense consequences, in conjunction with Christian theology, in generating a place for women in Western civilization quite different from that found in other cultures.

Everywhere we find kings seeking to extend their dominion over both neighbouring territories and their own vassals. And in this respect the story of freedom is one of institutions and laws which balanced the demands of the dominant powers in these small societies. The king of England as the fountainhead of justice had an officer of his own, called a sheriff, in each of the counties, and his judges travelled the country dispensing justice in response to an ever more flexible set of claims and petitions called writs. But the nobles in turn had the right to force an errant king to recognize a betrayal of his trust and to force him to make reparation. The most famous occasion of this sort was when King John was forced to affirm the Magna Carta at Runnymede in the Thames valley in 1215, and Magna Carta became enshrined in English legend as the source of English liberties. In fact this was not a unique medieval occasion, but one of the standard crises of medieval politics. And it illustrates a central feature of European development: rights and liberties were first elaborated by, and commonly in the interests of, the nobility and the richer inhabitants of the towns, and then only very slowly filtered down, over the generations, to lower levels of society. The voter of today, in other words, inherits the rights first sustained by the barons of old. Whatever the defects of this historical experience, it did have the consequence that the culture needed to sustain freedom had been thoroughly tested in custom and institution before the movement for democracy extended these rights to all. Democracy has thus emerged in European states out of an organic development which sustains it at a profound level.

The essence of medieval politics lay in the fact that the king could not rule – even to the extent of carrying out the very limited functions of rule as it was understood at that time – without the co-operation of partners. He had to consult the nobles, the magnates of the Church, and, in time, representatives from the towns who could make commitments of money. It was this situation which generated the quite new institution of parliaments. Parliaments have a complicated history, very different in each of the European realms. France, for example, had both *parlements* which were essentially legal institutions, and the Estates General (*états généraux*), which were consultative. Kings needed parliaments to agree taxation and sometimes to give weight to royal policy in international dealings. Subjects valued them as they offered an opportunity to influence the law and to secure remedies against the abuse of power. The history of the English parliament is perhaps the most complicated of all; it is also the most significant, in that parliamentary institutions fell into disuse in most of Europe in the early modern period, and were only revived as devices of liberal democracy in the nineteenth century on the model of what had so successfully survived in England. But what makes parliaments an almost pure example of political creativity is that they responded to the exigencies of the moment. Unplanned, they turned out to be the essential instruments of democracy, but it was quite late in the day that they provoked reflection on such abstract aspects of their operation as representation.

The third element of medieval politics is the most important of all. It concerns religion, which is the beliefs and feelings a civilization has about the point of being alive. The Greeks and Romans had enjoyed a civic religion, in which it made no sense to distinguish between membership of church and state: the same set of institutions covered both of the functions we in the West now so clearly distinguish. In classical times, the significance of a human life consisted in exhibiting rationality and serving the republic. With the rise of Christianity to a position of dominance in the Roman empire by the fourth century, we have a quite new religious situation. One had been born an Athenian or a Roman. Religion was part of the package. But one could only become a Christian by deliberately acquiring a set of beliefs. In addition, Christianity was a religion of the book, something which set a premium on education and literacy. Partly because of this it soon became so complicated a structure of beliefs, sentiments, injunctions, and rituals that it required a vast amount of intellectual reflection, including philosophizing, in order to make it a coherent whole. Beliefs are vulnerable things, requiring custodians of their purity or orthodoxy, for the human capacity to misunderstand, or perhaps understand all too well, is very considerable. The elaboration of Christian belief out of the relatively slight materials to be found in the New Testament was the work of church councils over several centuries, and in an important sense this work has never ceased. It began with the letters of St Paul in the first generation, and was continued throughout the early centuries of Christianity. By the death of St Augustine in AD 430, the basic structure (and an immense amount of intricate superstructure out of which heresies might be made) had been elaborated. This dangerously disruptive possibility of unorthodox belief is, of course, the source of much of the intolerance to be found in the history of Christianity, an intolerance of which the Inquisition has become an emblem. But it is also the source of much of the intellectual vitality of a Christian civilization.

Christianity was in these elaborations revealed to be a religion of moral challenge. Human beings were the workmanship of the creator of the universe. They had betrayed his trust by falling into sin but had been redeemed by the divine mission of Jesus. Human life was a time of trial and test, after which some people would have immortal life. Others, perhaps most, would suffer a different fate, and much thought was given to what it might be, the medieval elaboration of the torments of hell setting the tone of human life for centuries. What this religion meant was that each person was the custodian of his or her own soul and responsible for it to God. Death was no escape from this awful responsibility, for judgement continued beyond the grave. It affected great and humble alike. Greek and Roman religion and philosophy were, it will be remembered, highly élitist. Full humanity was only possible for the hero and the philosopher, while slaves, and to some extent women, were inferior specimens of an ideal. Christianity often reversed this judgement: it was the humble people who were closest to the spirit of love which God was thought to require. This particularly included women, who were enthusiastic about a faith preaching peace and love.

Some enthusiasts for ancient republics – Machiavelli and Nietzsche are examples of this line of thought – have taken this aspect of Christian belief as an enfeebling pietism hostile to the vitality and sense of honour found in the warrior. Whatever view we take of this, we must not conclude that the *respublica Christiana* of the Middle Ages was notably peaceful or obedient. The Church did indeed seek to encourage peace and humility among a tetchy and quarrelsome set of kings and aristocrats, but it also preached crusades, most of which aimed to take Jerusalem back from Islam by main force. However much the pulpit might echo to the reiteration of Romans 13, in which St Paul exhorts Christians to obey the powers that be, European life was notably turbulent and rebellious. The real significance Christianity had for political life lay in its transformation of human values.

Christianity affirmed the equal value in the sight of God of each human soul. And the value of each individual lay not in his or her participation in universal reason, but in a personality which responded to the challenge of sin. Philosophers found it difficult to give an account of this notion of personality, and tended to relapse back into the classical account of moral life as a contest between reason and the passions. But with the emergence of Protestantism at the Reformation in the sixteenth century, it was becoming clear to all, Protestant and Catholic alike, that modern human beings must be conceived of in terms of *will*, though not in any superficial sense which might identify will merely with getting one's way. Christianity turned human attention away from political conquest and the material things of the world towards the cultivation of the inner life, and the emergence of the modern world is the slow construction of a society in which that concern with the inner life could fully parallel involvement with the world. The modern world is, of course, a dynamic process, and individualism in this sense has perhaps long passed its peak, but its debris is still to be found around us, in popular books about how to attain happiness by inner fulfilment and in the popularity of the idea of human rights, which would not be conceivable except as the outcome of the tortuous journey of Christian theology.

The Christian religion transformed the Roman empire and allowed new spiritual shoots to grow amid the decay of its civil and military power. The Roman empire in the west turned itself into the Roman Catholic Church, Roman provinces becoming dioceses, the Pope rising in power as the Emperor declined, the Roman foundational myth of Romulus coming to be focused on Jesus as the founder of the City of God, and the distinctions of Roman law being exploited to make sense of the relations between the Old Testament and the revelation of Jesus. The holy texts guided life. Jesus had said: 'Thou art Peter, and upon this rock I shall build my Church' and the successors of St Peter as bishops of Rome built up a power which came to bestride the continent and in time the world. An alliance between this sacred power and that of the monarchs was forged by turning the inauguration of kingship into the religious ceremony of coronation. The Church turned marriage into a sacred as well as a merely social bond. By the eleventh century, the Pope could fight the most powerful of secular rulers on equal terms and control high affairs of state. Europe was spiritually governed by an absolute monarch whose agents were charged with the regulation of large areas of life. The very architecture of Europe was dominated by the vast cathedrals of the towns, and by the churches found in every village from the Mediterranean to the shores of the Baltic. In time, papal power overreached itself, the secular rulers reasserted themselves, and after 1309 the papacy spent many years at Avignon in the pocket of the king of France before returning in the following century to Rome. But it had indelibly affected the structure of European politics, becoming, along with the nobility, another power which kings had to balance as they constructed their realms.

Chapter 5
Constructing the Modern State

Take your choice where the medieval realm gives way to the modern state: most scholars choose the sixteenth century, but a century is a long time, and historians have often found supposedly feudal features of European life right up to the French Revolution and beyond. The 'modern state' is an umbrella term sheltering many different kinds of politics.

Religion is at the centre of the story. A grumbling of heresies in the later Middle Ages turned into fully fledged schism after 1517 when Luther defied the Pope by nailing his theses to the church door in Wittenberg. Religion determined politics because the most important thing in most lives was eternal salvation, and communities were reluctant to tolerate forms of belief unpleasing to God. The Reformation and counter-Reformation of the sixteenth century created immense spiritual enthusiasm, and much of the politics of England during this period concerned the martyrs who tried to save the country from heresy or, alternatively, prevent it from sinking back into popish superstition. And the political significance of these passions lies in the fact that the civil society of the time was conceived of as an association of believers. To reject fundamental communal beliefs was a kind of internal emigration.

The politics of the modern state emerged out of two conflicting movements: kingdoms tended to fragment in some ways, and to become unified in others. Centralizing monarchs acquired the concentrated powers of sovereignty, yet at the same time both individuals and established classes were able to entrench privileges and usages, some coming to be formulated in the emerging vocabulary of 'rights'.

In the earlier period, the nobles were an increasingly disorderly element. They constituted a warrior class with little to fight except each other, and throughout Europe civil war and local dissension threatened a reversion to primitive conditions. The Wars of the Roses in England during the thirty years before the coming of the Tudor monarchs in 1485 was largely power-hungry aristocratic opportunism, but the French wars of religion in the next century mingled aristocratic ambition and religious enthusiasm. The English civil war after 1642, and the contemporaneous Thirty Years War in Germany, have both sometimes been seen as part of the long transition from medieval localism to the centralized modern state. The common response to civil war is an enthusiasm for absolute government. It takes two or more to fight wars, and it seemed to make sense to concentrate all power in a sovereign ruler, conformity to whose laws would guarantee peace. Just such a ruler, however, might well misuse his power. It is clear that many feared the possibility of despotism. Thus Prince Hal, referring to the death of his father in Part 2 of Shakespeare's *Henry IV* reassuringly remarks:

> Brothers, you mix your sadness with some fear:
> This is the English, not the Turkish Court.

The new politics revolved around a court, and the court itself soon lost its medieval mobility and settled in one or more grand palaces which set the style for luxury and taste. A new kind of creature emerged: the courtier, whose aim was advancement and whose skill was to please. The nobility were assimilated into the court, and found that they had to become educated in order to retain their traditional role as the monarch's counsellors. It was a dangerous role. Treason laws flourished in the early modern period, and the grandees who played the power game were seldom more than a few steps away from the block. The danger was particularly great for those whose blood line made them possible candidates for the succession. Elizabeth I reluctantly assented to the execution of Mary Queen of Scots because alive she threatened to become a focus for Roman Catholic rebellion. Out in the wider world, public opinion stirred, especially in the cities, stimulated by the pamphlets and broadsheets which printing made possible. By the seventeenth century, this wider public was beginning to play an independent role in politics. Cromwell's army was full of remarkable men who had thought deeply about God and kings, and could express themselves in direct, pithy sentences, as they did in the Army Debates at Putney in 1647.

We rightly think of early modern court life as a sinister and melodramatic world – remembering those like Thomas More ('the king's good servant, but God's first'), Anne Boleyn, Lady Jane Grey, Essex, and many others whose ending on the block has inspired literary recapitulation. Staking one's life in the game of politics remained a deadly option until the beginning of the eighteenth century, since when only the melodrama of revolution has renewed the risk of death and imprisonment. Politicians in modern liberal democracies confidently expect to die in bed. In the modern world it is only despotisms which have recourse to the firing squad or the noose.

The high-risk politics of the early modern period resulted from the insecurity of rulers. In modern democracies, doctrine falsely suggests that rulers are basically in harmony with those they rule, but the very fact of authority necessarily distances the rulers from the ruled. Total intimacy and frankness is a dangerous indulgence for rulers, who are also in some degree at the mercy of the hopes and fears of those they rule. In a despotism this gulf is often recognized by construing the ruler as a god. The emergence of political activity quite specifically rejects this option, and the history of politics from one point of view is the exploration of expedients which minimize, even though they cannot eliminate, this distance between ruler and ruled. In the Greek *polis* and in republican Rome, for example, a certain public-spiritedness could be relied upon to give rulers and ruled a common basis for action. Again, in the medieval realm, the king was the leader of his vassals who in turn were responsible for those beneath them. Rule was a moral relationship. Kings engaged in the activity called 'policy' (which involved ruthlessness and dissembling) in relation to outside magnates, but in principle, at least, they had no need for 'policy' towards their peoples. With emerging modernity, however, it became necessary to practise 'policy' in managing one's own turbulent subjects. Many of these subjects were now literate and had very definite religious and political views of their own, which might well incline them to support a change of regime. The heterogeneity of an individualistic society, combined with the problem of keeping order in a large state by abstract laws, generated 'the new politics'.

The new politics first became explicit in the Italian cities where civic republics gave way to rule by tyrants – masterful adventurers who kept the peace by the exercise of unchecked power. By contrast with the medieval monarch, relatively secure in his rank and his religious status as the anointed of God, the *signore* had to be suspicious and wary. His insecure rule was always in danger from conspiracies or alliances that powerful families in his realm might make with neighbouring states. This 'art of the state' (as the new politics has been called) came in time to turn the traditional concern with justice into mere façade and to shift the focus to the cynical advice on how to keep power which had always been a part, but usually a subordinate part, of traditional accounts of the skill of ruling. A prince of this sort was now entirely given over to 'policy', perhaps the most important part of which were the devices of management to be used to keep his own subjects loyal to his interest. Machiavelli's *Prince* is a handbook of this art, and in time its precepts came to be summed up in Botero's formula as 'reason of state'.

Here then was an entirely new conception of politics, new at least in the thoroughness with which it was theorized. It was regarded by contemporaries sometimes as a form of realism ('the effective truth' of politics, as Machiavelli put it) and sometimes as the sign of corrupt and degenerate times. The standard by which this corruption might be measured was the tradition of the classical republic as defined by Cicero and handed down by many successors both in the later Roman world and in medieval times. In this conception of politics, the ruler's overriding concern was with justice and the encouragement of virtue throughout the city, for it was on virtue that peace and good order ultimately depended. The idea of a classical republic inspired a tradition of thought which, overtaken by the new politics of reason of state in early modern times, was preserved largely in the writings of philosophers, utopians, and pamphleteers. It survived to become endlessly transformed in the complex history of modern political thought. The ambiguous Machiavelli gave an account of this conception of the state in his *Discourses on the First Ten Books of Titus Livius*, and it spread. Nostalgia for a lost world of the republic was a counterpoint to the monarchical loyalty of the early modern period, and came to dominate Enlightenment criticism of the *ancien régime* in the eighteenth century. In republican terms, and in the opinion of many of the prudent middle classes, monarchy seemed wasteful, warlike, and exploitative, an affront to humanity. Indeed, the monarch seemed barely different from a tyrant. Thomas Hobbes had attacked this doctrine in *Leviathan* (1651), arguing that such idealism caused immense bloodshed in Europe by making young scholars the dupes of ambitious men.

Hobbes was responding to new problems. One of these was that religious dissension or aristocratic ambition could plunge a modern state into civil war. Another problem was the fact of individuality, for even individuals could come into destructive conflict with each other over religion, virtue, policy, and much else. It was indeed this very diversity of modern opinion (along with the fact that modern monarchies were too big to have the same kind of public life as city-states) which made the republican model in its classical form nothing but a seductive memory. The way Hobbes put this together was to argue that the only basic thing on which all men could agree was that death, and especially sudden death, was the supreme evil. His theoretical solution to these problems replicated much that had in fact been developing in practice: in each state, there must be a sovereign power with the authority to enforce the agreement necessary for a peaceful existence. The idea of sovereignty had previously been explored by the French lawyer Jean Bodin in his *Six Books of the Commonwealth* (1576). Sovereignty, said Bodin, was 'that absolute and perpetual power vested in a commonwealth which in Latin is termed *maiestas*'. But where Bodin based his state on families, Hobbes emphasized individuals torn between the passion for glory and the fear of death. The source of the sovereign's authority lay in the consent of the people themselves; indeed, they only became a people in the proper sense by appointing him as their representative.

The theory of sovereignty highlights one of the central problems of politics. It is universally agreed that freedom consists in living under law. But laws must be made. What then is the position of the lawmaker? If he is under the law, he cannot make it, and if he is above the law, then his subjects lack the security against oppression necessary for them to be free. Hobbes certainly agreed that the subjects of a modern state must be ruled by law, not by despotic caprice, but modern conditions require that rulers should have discretionary powers to deal with special situations. At this theoretical level, the problem cannot be solved. There is, in other words, always some element of risk in giving the necessary power to a sovereign authority. The practical argument is that the alternative is worse, for without sovereign power the subject has no protection against the aggression of others.

This logic reveals the bare bones of the extreme case. More confident peoples, or perhaps those who are merely insouciant about the dangers, might well think that the state might be based on the moral agreement of reasonable people, a package of moral prescriptions called natural law or (later) natural rights. This might solve the problem of the dangers of sovereignty. Hobbes's younger contemporary John Locke, in his *Two Treatises of Government* (1689), implicitly criticized Hobbes by deriding the idea of giving to any individual the total power to determine the rights of subjects; to do this would be 'to think that Men are so foolish that they take care to avoid what Mischiefs may be done them by *Pole-Cats*, or *Foxes*, but are content, nay think it Safety, to be devoured by *Lions*'.

Locke's confidence that men will agree about natural law made him insensitive to a problem which is at the heart of both the practice and the theory of modern government. The collisions between Thomas More and Henry VIII, between Chief Justice Coke and James I, and between the English parliament and Charles I all exemplify the perennial tension between what the ruler thinks the state needs and what the lawyers say the state will allow. The Watergate case which brought down President Nixon in the United States, and the doings of the Committee of Public Safety during the French Revolution offer highly disparate examples of the same basic tension. In practice, democracy and the separation of powers are among the ways in which the sovereign power has been transformed so that it may not exploit the power of the state. Concepts of natural law, rights, consent, nationalism, and the general will are theories which in one degree or another offer at least mitigation of the problem. But even in the best regulated of worlds, it has to be recognized that political power is necessary but dangerous stuff. No precautions can guarantee complete safety.

This problem became increasingly acute because modern technology constantly enhanced the actual power available to a ruler. Pen and ink allowed the development of a bureaucracy whose records exceeded the longest memory. Identities and passports could be issued and checked, frontiers drawn with accuracy on maps (as happened first at the Treaty of Westphalia in 1648). Explosives had rendered the fortresses of the nobility useless, and censorship and control of printing helped rulers to determine in some degree the ideas available to their subjects. But it will be obvious that the bearing on politics of modern technology ebbs and flows in accordance with our themes of unification and fragmentation. The power of governments may well have been enhanced by the technology of surveillance available during the late nineteenth and first half of the twentieth century, but more recently, tourism, computers, and geographical mobility have produced the opposite effect.

It will already be clear that the modern state has turned the whole idea of politics upside down, and that this has happened in response to religious change. Men in classical times found in service to the state what most satisfied their natures. Modern Europeans, as individuals concerned above all about salvation, have often taken the function of the state as merely to ensure the peace necessary for their own projects. The liberal view of the state is just a secular version of this attitude. One might expect such governments to be weak and divided, but in fact the modern state has been remarkably tough and durable. The German philosopher Hegel indulged in hyperbole when in his *Philosophy of Right* (1821) he characterized the state as 'the march of God on earth', but he expressed prophetically the sense of a link between the state and cosmic destiny which has been felt by many Europeans since his time, and has proved itself in the mass wars of the last two centuries.

Out of the ramshackle realms of the Middle Ages, then, there came into being a dazzling new piece of institutional machinery called 'the state' – so dazzling that it has swept the world. It represented the nearest thing to omnipotence human beings could construct, and, in a technological world, it soon became the focus of dreams. What faults in the human condition could it not, properly understood, remedy? Two contrasting attitudes reveal the rhythm of modern politics. The first is the liberal view of the state, descending from medieval conceptions of freedom and kingship, as sustaining a civic order to be enjoyed. The second is the art of the state as something repressive, standing over against the aspirations of its exploited subjects, the state as a problem because it is a repressive thing that needs to be humanized. And this second view has given rise to the aspiration to transcend the state altogether and create a perfect republic in which the gap, inevitable in politics, between ruler and subject has been entirely closed. Modern politics is in large measure a dialogue between these alternatives.

Chapter 6
How to Analyse a Modern Society

How should we visualize a modern state? The more complicated the world becomes, the harder it is. But we may approach the problem by remembering that most civil associations, when they weren't ships of state being steered, have been bodies politic. Political associations must have a head, or ruler, to govern, and arms, or warriors, with which to defend themselves. Counsellors are deliberative, messengers the nerves, and agriculture the belly of this complex body, as the Roman patrician Menenius Agrippa argued when (as Plutarch tells it) he persuaded angry farmers that they must not rebel against the senatorial head. Shakespeare often used this image of the body politic, and illustrates the point with another, musical, metaphor, in the famous words he gives Ulysses in *Troilus and Cressida:*

> Take but degree away, untune that string
> And hark what discord follows. Each thing meets
> In mere oppugnancy.

The image of the state as a body conveyed that it was a unified corporate structure, in which each element must play its part in an overall harmony. Individuals and groups within the state were meaningless except as the creatures of their society. The relation of part to whole, as St Thomas Aquinas put it, was that of imperfect to perfect.

43

Christianity was an earthquake which shook the foundations of this conception of civil harmony, but the remarkable thing is that for fifteen hundred years the ruined classical structure stayed in place. Following Machiavelli, we have noted that the tension between the ideal of civil harmony on the one hand, and the rather turbulent adversarial practices of public life in Greece and Rome on the other, were one source of liberty. Yet the ideal of harmonious obedience never quite capitulated to the realistic view that the modern state is an equilibrium of divergent forces. Christianity exploited the idea of harmony even while also undermining it, partly by demoting politics to a merely temporal instrument for sustaining peace and worldly justice, and partly by making the care of each individual soul the fundamental thing in life.

Christianity taught Europeans to live within a divided society, and some of them have been trying to restore the lost unity ever since. The individual Christian found himself part of not one but two corporate bodies, the Church and the civil community, *sacerdotium* and *regnum*. Medieval law was also remarkably fluent in responding to an active and vigorous population by establishing further legal bodies, such as guilds and universities, of which the individual was a part. These bodies within bodies, as it were, accustomed Europeans to the transformations of modernity. The new sovereign state, while from one point of view simply an assemblage of equal subjects under a sovereign, was also a complex, highly articulated body.

The essence of modernity lay in the development of this new sentiment of individuality: the disposition increasingly to guide one's life by one's own talents and inclinations rather than to fill the place into which one had been born. The pioneering work of individualism was done in the sphere of religion, where pursuing one's inclinations – here decked out in the drapery of a newish thing called 'conscience' – was less a right than a duty. The Reformation left many people stranded under rulers who imposed a religion unacceptable to their inclinations, and they migrated. Some, like the Pilgrim Fathers, set up completely new societies which could reflect in full measure what they took to be right, while others tried to turn England, or Scotland, or the Swiss states into godly places according to their lights. But other inclinations, such as to make money, or risk one's fortune, or go soldiering, or devote one's life to art, were also part of this dissolution of traditional stabilities. It was particularly in the cities that individuals came to insist on pursuing their own inclinations. The climax of this movement came in the nineteenth century, when millions of Europeans, shopping, as it were, for the kind of state that best suited them, emigrated to the New World. Just such a pursuit of opportunity built the Americas, but even more significant was the drift all over the Western world from the countryside to the cities.

These mobile and self-dependent individuals could no longer plausibly be seen as merely contributory parts of one single body of activity. They were certainly subjects and citizens, but they also had private lives of their own, and a great number of social activities for which the state was merely an umbrella. In the early modern period, then, state and society came explicitly to be distinguished. Aristotle had defined man as a political animal, but already for Aquinas in the thirteenth century, man was political *and social*. By the seventeenth century most social contract theorizing distinguished the beginnings of society on the one hand from the construction of the state on the other. Society could even be imagined as an autonomous mode of association.

Society, then, was born out of the *state*. It was by no means the last type of association to detach itself from the state by such a process of abstraction. The growth of European commerce revealed that human beings also played roles as producers, distributors, and consumers of commodities. In this role, they often seemed like puppets on the strings of price. Money had often seemed to political philosophers a potential source of corruption, while rulers had given much thought to ways of extracting it from their subjects. By the eighteenth century, it became possible to think of individuals not merely as subjects, or as social beings, but also as participating in another distinct associative relationship: political economy, or more simply, the *economy*.

The remarkable thing about the economy was that it seemed to be a system largely independent of the will of the participants. In this respect, it interestingly resembled nature as it was coming to be revealed by science, and was strikingly different from social and political life, in which unpredictable human decisions were the rule. The movements of economic quantities were determinate, at least in principle. When the price of a commodity rose, consumers bought less of it, which tended to bring the price down again. Commodities in short supply infallibly rose in price so long as demand remained constant. There flashed upon the minds of some thinkers the idea that here, in economics, was to be found the key to a real science of man. The great Isaac Newton had demonstrated that the earth was a planet moving in a solar system according to exact laws. In 1776, Adam Smith published *The Wealth of Nations*, which exhibited the economy as a system of abstractions behaving in a similarly law-governed way.

Since this new system of relations resembled the Greek household writ large, it was called an 'economy' from the Greek *oikos*. The modern economy was called 'political' in order to distinguish it from the ancient household, and its great achievement was not only its rising prosperity but the fact that this was achieved by free labour, not by slaves – something which many were soon to regard as evidence for the morally progressive character of European civilization. Progress was the result of reason, which could analyse the processes of production into ever simpler component parts, the mechanization of some and the repetitive performance of others yielding great gains in efficiency. Early economists gloried in this achievement without being carried away by its possibilities. They knew about diminishing returns to all improvements, and the speculations of the Reverend Thomas Malthus, according to which most populations were doomed to live at around subsistence level, gave economics a dismal reputation. What was actually to transform the human condition was the accident of a highly rational and inventive collection of people in England finding themselves on top of large coal reserves. Water and wind merely supplemented human muscle, but coal-power set in motion the progress towards a push-button world. The genie of limitless human possibility had been released, and there is no doubt that it inflamed the minds of those who thought about politics.

In particular, it was the sovereign powers of Europe which saw in technological advance ways of pursuing their central project of increasing the extent of their dominions. This project primarily led them to chance their fortunes in war, a hobby which often led to national bankruptcy. The policy of national aggrandizement suggested that trade between nations was a competition for the acquisition of wealth. International trade was seen, in the jargon of a later period, as a zero-sum game: anything I win must be your loss. States therefore tried to monopolize trade, keep industrial techniques secret, protect their industries from competition, and rationalize the nation's productive resources, including human capital. This application of reason to economic competition was called mercantilism, and it was not a great success. It so happened that the British, whose dynasty was less able to impose central direction upon trade, also grew richer faster than anyone else. They increasingly left commerce unregulated, following the principles elaborated by Adam Smith according to which trade benefits both parties.

By the end of the eighteenth century, then, Europeans had learned to understand themselves as subjects and citizens in the state, as members of classes, institutions, religions, or status groups in society, and as producers and consumers in the economy. They were also beginning to learn that they were the bearers of a *culture*. Rationalism had taught them to regard themselves as part of humanity, possibly sharing in what were soon to be called 'the rights of man', but now romanticism made

47

them take notice of the fact that each people spoke a specific language or dialect, enjoyed particular culinary tastes, customs, manners, artistic inheritance, and much else. A culture was a kind of spiritual rather than political body (the German word *Volksgeist* hit the nail on the head) which expressed itself in poetry and song and was a unique modification of human possibility. The larger states at this time equipped themselves with national artists – Dante for the Italians, Cervantes for the Spaniards, Rabelais and Racine for the French, and Shakespeare for the English. Smaller cultures sometimes had to fit themselves up with this apparatus from scratch: devoted teachers wrote down and formalized the language, artists created literature and images, and historians a national legend.

The modern body politic thus turns out to be not one but a number of bodies. If we add mind, as constitutive of psychology, then in state, society, economy, and culture we have the conceptual ground-plan of the social sciences. Each association, as a concept, sustains a vast superstructure of theory and classification. But our concern is rather with the fact that these self-conscious associations set the scene for the dramas of modern political conflict. They provide a grid from which many powerful theories of politics can be constructed.

Until the economy and the state have been distinguished, for example, there can be no modern theory of socialism, which is a reflection on the relation between politics and the economy. Again, until culture had been distinguished from society, nationalism would have made no sense. Nationalism is the doctrine (espoused by figures as various as Mazzini and Woodrow Wilson, and animating such peoples as the Czechs, Serbs, Irish, Basques, and Bretons) that every culture ought to be self-determining. This doctrine must be distinguished from the sloppy usage of 'nationalism' to signify the passionate solidarity of established states in their quarrels with others of their kind – a quite different phenomenon. This confusion has yielded the mistaken theory that, since all conflict is caused by nationalism, the way to peace lies through the abandonment of national sovereignty in favour of the rule of international authorities.

Those who theorize these abstract associations are also tempted to simplify them by supplying a single dominant motive for each. *Homo politicus* for example is driven by power, *homo economicus* by the selfish desire for wealth. Society (sometimes shadowed by the rather more sentimental term 'community') stands for solidarity, the economy for division. It should not need to be emphasized that the whole range of human motives is in fact at play across the whole spectrum of modern association: power gets entangled with culture, idealism with politics, sport with economics, and so on. Fallacies arising from simple identifications of motive and association have long rampaged through both the theory and the practice of modern life, and this is no place to analyse them. One central point may, however, be made.

It concerns the expression 'self-interest', which has a complicated history, and within the moral structure of modern life refers not to the moral vice of selfishness but to the *duty* which an individualist society imposes upon its members to be self-moving and to avoid becoming a burden on others for their needs and resources. For some people, of course, this is impossible, and for many reasons, but unless most people were capable of behaving in this kind of self-interested way, modern societies would change into something different. Self-interest, of course, in no way excludes or conflicts with our duties to be considerate and helpful to our neighbour and to others with whom we come in contact. Indeed, unless we are independently self-moving we can be of little use to them.

Can we argue that any one of the four forms of association is more fundamental than the others? This is perhaps the founding question of modern political philosophy. The more profound thinkers such as Hobbes and Hegel, in their very different ways, insist that the state is fundamental as the condition of all else. It was against this view that

49

Karl Marx revolted, in making economics the determiner of the course of politics, and in absorbing everything into an extended sense of the term 'society'. It was Marx who most spectacularly explored one intellectually irresistible possibility arising from the grid we have described: namely, the idea that one or other of these associations *determines* the others. 'The mode of production of material life', wrote Marx in 1859, 'determines the social, political and intellectual life process in general.' He went on to claim that the material transformation of the economic conditions of production 'can be determined with the precision of natural science'. The search for this knowledge, if it exists, has been the philosopher's stone of modern social science, and we are nowhere nearer finding it. Some sceptics believe it is not there to be found.

A certain unreality haunts those political activists who argue that some other form of association is more fundamental than the state. This results from the paradox that what they actually seek is the power of the state in order to embark on a programme of social, or cultural, or economic transformation of the very spheres which their theory proclaims to be more fundamental than the state itself. If the superficial can determine the fundamental, something goes awry with our theory. The paradox finds its practical expression in such events as communists creating absolute power instead of abolishing the state they purport to regard as a mere façade, or African nationalists speaking on behalf of non-existent nations in order to become the government which will impose the cultural uniformity that actually *creates* the nation on whose behalf they purported to act in the first place.

All of these strange endeavours respond to a nostalgic yearning for the return of the unified body politic from which the modern state emerged. Classical republicans resented Christianity because it divided allegiance between secular and civil authorities, socialists thought that we were all torn apart between the individualistic imperatives of the workplace and communal allegiance to the state, nationalists that our cultural identity had been muddied by the oppression of alien rulers, and so on. The concept of alienation is one influential diagnosis of what ails us, and a great deal of modern politics is the doomed attempt to put Humpty Dumpty together again.

Chapter 7

Relations between States: How to Balance Power

However internally complex states may be, they face each other as unities armed and ready for both attack and defence. The history of Europe has largely been a story of war.

The reason is that so far no peaceful and prosperous social condition has long survived without the means of defending itself. A Europe of large and small political units has been an arena of wars, and they have generally been inconclusive. No state has long managed to dominate the rest. European history has been plausibly summed up as preparing for war, waging war, or recovering from war. One might have expected Christianity, as a religion of peace, to have modified this history, but its actual influence is perhaps best exemplified in the story told of Clovis, the leader of the West Franks, who conquered Gaul in AD 491 and was converted to Christianity. Listening one day to a sermon about the crucifixion, he could not help rising up in anger and bursting out: 'That would not have happened if I had been there with my Franks!' Morality can lead to war, no less than its opposite.

War kills people and destroys property, and rationalists blame it on the passions. Why in that case is the history of a rational species so dismal a tale? Part of the explanation is necessity. Since defeat in war could mean extinction as a people, and since there were always some states that were, or might become, expansionist, warriors were everywhere needed for protection. These warriors had an ethic of honour. Valour in battle was glorious and sacrifice would win, as it seemed, undying glory. In the millennium between the end of Rome in the west and the beginning of the modern world, these aristocratic protectors were to become the problem rather than the solution to the desire for peace. The death and destruction resulting from their feuding was brought to an end by the ascendancy of absolute monarchs, who then themselves became the source of the problem. War was now the pastime of kings; cannons, ran the motto, are the arguments of princes. By marriage and diplomacy, but above all by war, a state could grow to be a power. Over several centuries, the mosaic of small dominions inherited from the Middle Ages was consolidated by these means into the relatively simple political map of the Europe we know today.

War, as Clausewitz put it, is the continuation of policy – that is, politics – by other means. Rulers attack for advantage, and defend to protect the national interest. As in chess, one side or other must win, and even stalemate is merely a precarious equilibrium. To lose this international game may be a desperate thing, as the Poles discovered when the feebleness of their government left them to the partitioning mercies of the Russians, Prussians, and Austrians, and as many states discovered when overrun by Nazi Germany after 1939.

The best explanation of political conflict was given by Thomas Hobbes in *Leviathan* (1651). Hobbes called any situation in which men do not acknowledge a common superior a 'state of nature' and his thesis was that a state of nature is always a state of war, in which the life of man would be 'nasty, poor, solitary, brutish and short'. As he put it in the famous thirteenth chapter: 'men have no pleasure, but on the contrary a great deal of grief, in keeping company, where this is no power able to over-awe them all.' Hobbes suggested three basic reasons for this. We have already mentioned two of them: the scarcity of the things men value (such as well-watered land), and the human passion for glory. The third was something Hobbes called 'diffidence' or mistrust of others.

The very fear of the future aggression of others might well lead to a policy of pre-emptive strikes, which have a terrifying logic: Alpha fears that Beta will attack, and decides to strike first, but Beta already fears this, and wants to get in even earlier, fearing which Alpha . . . and so on.

Human beings living in a state of nature, and fearing death, must form a civil association by authorizing some superior power to rule them by law – an outcome Hobbes thought would most commonly come about through conquest. Human beings were impelled to take this course of action by their vulnerability. The situation of states is not essentially different; all that *is* different is the fact that states can protect themselves, whereas solitary individuals cannot. As Hobbes put it: 'in all times, kings and persons of sovereign authority, because of their independency, are in continual jealousies, and in the state and posture of gladiators; having their weapons pointing, and their eyes fixed on one another; that is, their forts, garrisons, and guns upon the frontiers of their kingdoms; and continual spies upon their neighbours; which is a posture of war.'

We can never quite escape the insecurities of the Hobbesian state of nature, which can be illustrated by the Wild West, or the condition of inner cities, the fear of footsteps when alone in a dark street at night, or (in an image used by Hobbes) by the fact that we lock our doors. And it is a powerful explanatory model because Hobbes had turned the whole question of war and peace upside-down. It had long been common to deplore war and seek its causes, as if it were a pathology to be explained. Hobbes argued that war was the natural relation between humans, and the real question was thus how they could ever achieve a condition of peace.

Broadly speaking, this model explains how European states have generally related to each other. Special circumstances may induce modifications: for example, the dominance of the USA and the USSR during much of the second half of the twentieth century made war between west European states seem unthinkable. In human affairs, however, nothing remains stable for long, and the interesting question is how Europe (by contrast with most other parts of the world) has for centuries been divided into separate and rather hostile states, none of which has long succeeded in subduing the rest.

What one would rather expect is that some conqueror would extend his power until problems of communications and logistics made further conquest unprofitable. This is what Rome did, and, notably, China and it illustrates a powerful logic in human affairs.

The millionaire who, when asked 'How much money is enough?' replied 'Just a bit more' recognized a central feature of human life. There are positive reasons why power tends to snowball, or why to those that hath it shall be given. Movements grow because everyone seeks to join up with power and success – known as the bandwagon effect. In the internal politics of some states, bandwagons work because after a certain point it becomes dangerous *not* to have joined. This makes democratic government in such states impossible, for the natural terminus is a single dominant party. But it is the negative reasons for the growth of power which are most striking. They are illustrated by the familiar board game called Monopoly in which the most successful capitalist ends up buying out his bankrupted competitors. This was how Karl Marx imagined capitalism. Similarly, no state is really secure until all of its competitors have been reduced to impotence or clienthood. The logic seems irresistible, but it turns out to be wrong. Why?

In the case of economics, it doesn't work because the economy is not a zero-sum game. Technology changes, large firms lose their flexibility, new ideas sweep all before them, and any theory of human life as a system with a logic of its own (such as Marxism) must fail. In a modern economy, which is a positive-sum game, everyone gets richer. Some, no doubt, get very much richer than others, but all enjoy cleaner water, more food, better health care, and other benefits. Let us now consider why the logic of Monopoly has so far failed to generate a single imperial power ruling all Western Europe.

The reason lies in the balance of power. Our logic of human endeavour does indeed work in explaining the fact that a succession of potential unifiers of Europe have arisen, but in each case they have been frustrated by the propensity of other European states to unite in frustrating the ambitious hegemon. In the sixteenth century, Habsburg Spain, buoyed up by gold from the New World, bestrode the Continent, but found itself blocked by Valois France. By the late seventeenth century, it was Louis XIV of France who threatened the independence of his neighbours, especially Holland, which was led by the indomitable William III (as he became when in 1689 he was crowned king of England). When in 1700 it seemed as if the Bourbons might control both France and Spain, all Europe united against Louis, and his armies suffered numerous defeats at the hands of John Churchill, Duke of Marlborough. During the eighteenth century, Russia, Prussia, and Austria were major players in this game. Even tiny Sweden had nearly a century of world-historical significance before the adventures of Charles XII exhausted her resources. After the French Revolution, it was Napoleon whose bid for world power united everyone against him. The history of the twentieth century has been dominated by the policy of blocking the hegemony which Germany's power and population demanded. Power has thus always found its balance, but the costs have been great. That is why so many Europeans have favoured transposing this whole endeavour into a new key, and creating a unified Europe by agreement rather than conquest.

European unity might at least change a situation in which the ally of one epoch may become the enemy of the next, a fact which illustrates the essential coldness and brutality of much politics. We often construe inter-state relations in terms of the metaphor of friends and foes, but misleadingly. A great power, as many statesmen have said, has no friends, merely interests, and interests change. 'Blood dries quickly' remarked Charles de Gaulle, and countries do indeed rapidly forget the enmities of yesteryear. The idea of friendship in international politics is merely sentimental overlay concealing calculations of national interest. But what is national interest?

It is whatever a state judges necessary to its security. Control of the Suez Canal was a British national interest so long as Britain ruled India; not afterwards. A national interest is limited by reality. The Poles would certainly prefer not to have such powerful and difficult neighbours as Germany and Russia, but it is not open to choice. The United States could promulgate a Monroe Doctrine largely declaring the hemisphere out of bounds to European interventions, but its power to do so has not always pleased its neighbours to the south. Thomas Jefferson was deeply suspicious of France just before the Louisiana Purchase of 1803, remarking: 'The day that France takes possession of New Orleans . . . we must marry ourselves to the British fleet and nation.' Neighbours are commonly enemies, while neighbours-but-one are allies.

The national interest is a matter of interpretation, but changes of regime seldom greatly change a state's idea of its national interest. Revolutionary France after 1789 and Bolshevik Russia after 1917 largely continued the foreign policies of their predecessors, but were additionally aggressive. Sometimes the national interest acquires the dignity of a theory to sustain it, as in Cardinal Richelieu's doctrine that the Alps, Pyrenees, and the Rhine formed the natural frontiers of France. Judgements of national interest require prudence, and some concern for the likely trend of future events. Consider as typical of such reasoning, Winston Churchill reflecting on Britain's national interest in the early 1920s:

> It is argued that we could never endure the possession of the Channel
> ports by a victorious Germany . . . We dwelt, however, for centuries
> when those same Channel ports were in the possession of the greatest
> European military power, when that power – France – was almost

unceasingly hostile to us. It is said that new weapons aggravate the danger. But that depends on who has the best and most powerful weapons. If, in addition to sea supremacy, we had air supremacy, we might maintain ourselves as we did in the days of Napoleon for indefinite periods, even when all the Channel ports and all the Low Countries were in the hands of a vast hostile military power. It should never be admitted in this argument that England cannot, if worse comes to worst, stand alone. I decline to accept as an axiom that our fate is involved in that of France.

The cold logic of politics requires that men and wealth should be sacrificed to protect the national interest. This necessity has always been known. In modern times it generated the idea of reason of state which may require violence, deception, and the breaking of promises. As Hobbes remarked, in war, force and fraud are the cardinal virtues, and he regarded international relations as always potentially a condition of war. Cavour, one of the creators of a united Italy in the nineteenth century, is reported as remarking: 'What scoundrels we would be if we had done for ourselves what we have done for our country.'

Yet in more recent times reason of state has been remembered largely for its failures, because these failures reinforce the case for the international morality which has grown up as a countervailing movement to the untrammelled power of national sovereignty. When Napoleon sent troops across the border into Baden to capture and shoot the duc d'Enghien, an act which shocked the whole of Europe, Talleyrand remarked. 'It was worse than a crime, it was a blunder.' And the German Chancellor Bethmann Hollweg is denigrated for his remark at the start of the First World War that the 1839 treaty guaranteeing the integrity of Belgium (which Germany had just violated) was only 'a scrap of paper'.

The movement to turn the society of European states into an international moral order derives from the medieval idea of

Christendom, which in turn owed much to the Romans and the philosophy of natural law. The Romans had a law covering relations between peoples (the *ius gentium*), while philosophers had followed the Stoics in exploring the rational precepts of a law of nature which applied to all human beings. War within the common culture of Christendom acquired usages and conventions which in some small degree mitigated its ferocity: heralds, ambassadors, signs of truce, and conventions for the treatment of prisoners of war and the immunity of civilians, including, more recently, the immunities of the Red Cross. Some rationalists of the eighteenth century were self-conscious cosmopolitans who detached themselves from loyalty to their state, and some dreamed of a universal republic that would bring peace to the world. Not all philosophers shared the dream. Hegel, for example, while not defending war, observed that it was the nursery of the heroic virtues.

The study of international relations is riven by a conflict between realists, who take the national interest as their guide, and idealists, who focus on the emergence of an international order. The idealist case has a broad popular appeal. It takes the view that if war ever was a rational way to settle conflicts, it ceased to be so with the emergence of weapons of mass destruction. Another powerful argument is that irresistible developments, especially in trade, have made countries so interdependent that the sovereignty of national states is an illusion. An application of this argument is that environmental policies for the planet require international action. The process of globalization has certainly incorporated all of mankind within an international system of states, including the world-wide currency of human rights, particularly the rights of women, which are especially disruptive in traditional societies. Some non-Western societies reject the attempt to impose such rights as a form of Western cultural imperialism. A global economy is certainly emerging, but equally certainly there is no emergence of a dominant global morality.

The moral thrust of internationalism is to identify the national interest with selfishness. Conformity to international treaties and the implementation of rights is, by contrast, seen as virtuous. The reader will already have realized, however, that nothing in politics is purely moral, or indeed purely economic, spiritual, or anything else. What is economically efficient may be spiritually destructive, and what is universally moral may be fatal to a specific culture. It is not even as if the movement for international virtue can claim to be entirely independent of particular interests. International morality certainly suits some nations more than others, and a prosperous bureaucracy of civil servants with clients among the pressure-groups of Western countries benefits from its extension.

Realists claim that national interest remains, and indeed ought to remain, the lodestar of international relations. They have seen a whole succession of monocausal theories of the causes of war (baronial arrogance, dynastic ambition, nationalism, or fanaticism) refuted by the facts. Their concern is that utopian aspirations towards a new peaceful world order will simply absolutize conflicts and make them more intractable. National interests are in some degree negotiable; rights, in principle, are not. International organizations such as the United Nations have not been conspicuously successful in bringing peace, and it is likely that the states of the world would become extremely nervous of any move to give the UN the overwhelming power needed to do this. International relations is thus one area which conspicuously demonstrates that all political solutions tend to create new political problems.

Chapter 8

The Experience of Politics:
I. How to be an Activist

Those who study politics are called political scientists, and we must presently consider politics as a science. First, however, we must look to what it is that scientists have to study: namely, the actual experience of engaging in politics.

This experience is sometimes compared to theatre. Politicians and actors certainly belong to related tribes. Much of the architecture of public life recalls the Classical inspiration of the Roman forum, especially that of Washington. In London, the Houses of Parliament, rebuilt in the middle of the nineteenth century, have been appropriately described as 'a basically classical structure with neo-Gothic detail'. The architecture of the Kremlin and its communist embellishments reflect the remoteness and grandiosity of despotism. French public architecture is imperial in its grandeur. That the British prime minister lives in a more or less ordinary house in a more or less ordinary street reveals something of the studied casualness of British public life.

These are the national theatres of politics, but most political drama, even in a televisual age, takes place in local and regional offices, in dusty halls and on windy street corners where electors can be harangued. Politics has its own logistics: it requires agents, premises, contacts with printers, a pool of supporters, money, and generally, as the condition of all these things, an established political party. The rich and famous are sometimes inclined to start a party from scratch, but it is a difficult option. The typical route taken by the ambitious politician is from the periphery to the centre, and each step of the way resembles a game of snakes and ladders.

The politician needs, for a start, the same kind of knowledge as the concerned citizen; just more of it. What American politician could move a step without a close knowledge of the Constitution, the Bill of Rights, and many of the decisions of the Supreme Court? Knowledge of history is indispensable, supplying a range of memories, references, and metaphors without which political talk is unintelligible. From the War of Independence, through the Civil War, to the very songs and slogans of the American past, the politician must be able to pick up the references, many of them highly local, which constitute the culture of those whom he seeks to represent. He must know how the Senate and Congress work in detail, not to mention the way in which the states relate to them. Much of this is low-level, slightly tedious, descriptive material, but without it the politician's understanding hardly rises above gossip.

Traditions of politics vary greatly. In beginning by contrasting politics with despotism, we have already suggested that there is an immense gulf dividing the possible ways of ordering a society. The very idea of what a human being is, and what is due to men, and especially to women, will in many countries be remote from what is believed by the average reader of this book. A tradition is something 'handed down' from one generation to another, and (perhaps re-described as 'political culture') must be the central object of understanding in any political system. It is composed of many strands, and what people say about the state may give very little sense of the reality of politics. A population long accustomed to being exploited by tax collectors, for example, has an attitude to the census, to governmental forms, and the rhetoric of leaders quite different from that which used to be found in European liberal democracies. In some traditions, people are sanguine about what can be changed, in others cynical and fatalistic. The very language in which the thoughts and sentiments pass down over the generations reveals a conceptual structure which affects political possibility. All languages have some analogue for 'justice', for example, but there are many variations on this broad theme – such as the idea of fairness – which can only be imported from other languages. Even European languages which are culturally similar to English do not yield a genuine translation of the subtitle – *Justice as Fairness* – of John Rawls's *A Theory of Justice*. Again, the Chinese character for 'freedom' connotes slipperiness and egoism rather than the courage and independence with which Europeans associate the term.

Most political knowledge generalizes experience. The politician cannot help but learn a great deal from the past, and especially from exemplary heroes and villains. Machiavelli recommended a close attention to the great deeds of ancient Rome, but modern history is not a whit less fertile in suggestive examples, and certainly much more revealing about our own political traditions. A British politician, for example, must know something of Magna Carta, Roundhead and Cavalier, Whig and Tory, the Reform Bills of the nineteenth century, the contrasting political styles of prime ministers such as Melbourne, Peel, Disraeli, Gladstone, Churchill, Attlee, and Wilson, not to mention the events of the twentieth century. Much of this will be legend, and what is heroic to some will be deplorable to others. A Labour politician might regard Ramsay MacDonald's formation of the National Government in 1931 as an act of treason to the party; a Conservative would treat the event quite differently, and would certainly see it as less important. Politicians train for the real world by endless talk about past landmarks and present possibilities, and they do so in a special language of their own. Thus 'appeasement' is no longer in politics the name of a type of response to someone's discontent, but refers to a dispute about foreign policy in the 1930s. For several decades after the Second World War it denoted an episode of shame and cowardice. Then came revision, an attack on the reputation of Churchill, the great critic of appeasement, and the argument that Britain's lone stand against Hitler in 1940 had merely delivered her into the hands of the rising empires of the USA and the USSR. It is very seldom that events stand still for long, and the paradox is that the past is nearly as opaque as the future.

For the aspiring politician in a country such as France, the past hangs more heavily than it commonly has in Anglo-Saxon countries. The French Revolution split France profoundly, largely along religious and secular lines, and the Nazi occupation left memories which determined political allegiances for the rest of the century. Irish politics has been similarly haunted by memory. The United States has, in general, been more fortunate, though the legacy of the Civil War has been bitter.

Since politics is talk, political skill requires wit, and politicians are remembered for their phrases. Winston Churchill is remembered both for the speeches which articulated 'the lion's roar' during the Second World War and for a string of witticisms, some of them malicious, like his description of Clement Attlee as 'a sheep in sheep's clothing'. Lincoln's political success came from his wisdom, but it is hard to imagine his political skill without his dazzling capacity for oratory. These men all belong, of course, to a vanished time when citizens attended like connoisseurs to long and complicated political speeches. Gladstone once took four hours to introduce his budget to the House of Commons – fortified, it is said, with raw eggs and sherry. That culture has been destroyed by the trivializing effect of radio and television, which provide such abundant distraction for the mind that politics must be fitted into a much smaller space: the 'sound-bite'. The sound-bite belongs to the simplified world of the slogan and the banner, but this does not diminish the need of the politician for the phrasemaker.

In modern democracies, a politician is a spokesman for some broadly based opinion, and what he or she hopes to become is the holder of an office. *Spokesmanship* and *office* are the polarities within which the men and women who go in for politics must live, and each reveals much about politics.

Spokesmanship is representation, and modern government must be conducted by representatives rather than by the citizens themselves because legislative enactments, often some hundreds of pages long, are too complicated to be mastered without unusual skill and attention. But the representative function of the politician begins long before policies emerge. It is the skill of constructing a position which will appeal to many people because it can harmonize conflicting desires. The superficial critic of politicians can see the vagueness and indeterminacy which are certainly often necessary for this, but generally fails to appreciate the trick of finding some essence of an issue that can unite different opinions. A skilful politician resembles a magician in his capacity to set an object before the mind of one audience, while keeping it invisible to others, sometimes in the same hall. Simple-minded rationalists sometimes stigmatize this characteristic of politicians as nothing but support-seeking duplicity, and journalists have taken to 'decoding' their speeches and disclosing the supposed 'message' behind the words. Better understood, this technique is the tact which allows people with very different judgements and preferences to live together in one society; where it fails – as, for example, in the difficulty Canadian politicians have had in projecting a 'Canada' that would accommodate Francophone and Anglophone opinion – then society moves to the brink of dissolution. American politicians finessed the division over slavery for as long as they could, for they suspected that the real alternative was civil war, and they were right.

Constrained by his representative function, the politician is further circumscribed by the responsibilities of his *office*. The raw brutalities of power are largely converted into the suavities of authority, and it is important to distinguish these two phenomena. The outsider is often impressed by the power of those who hold important positions in the state, but power, while attractive as a kind of melodrama, is mostly exaggerated. The office of a prime minister or president is constitutionally limited, and idealists quickly find that their capacity to improve the world requires whole streams of concessions they would prefer not to make. As Harry S. Truman remarked: 'About the biggest power the President has is the power to persuade people to do what they ought to do without having to be persuaded.' The power of an office is merely the skill by which a ruler can use his authority to get the right things done. Otherwise, when people talk of 'power' they merely mean the pleasure an office-holder may get from a purely personal exercise of will, which is basically a trivial thing. Most trivial of all is the pleasure in being the constant focus of attention in public places, and the capacity to please – but also to frustrate – the ambitious people by whom the politician is surrounded. It can no doubt be exploited for illicit purposes. President Kennedy notoriously used his prestige as president to induce large numbers of women to sleep with him, though since he was also handsome and rich, he hardly needed presidential prestige for that. It may be that, like the kinds of political groupie the Hungarian writer Arthur Koestler talked about, some of them 'wanted to sleep with history'. Such power is not a thing possessed by the power-holder, but a moral relationship between the power-holder and the person over whom the power is supposedly exercised. Where it is a form of corruption, it involves the corruption of both parties.

The fact that persuasion lies at the heart of politics has one central implication: the reasons a politician decides upon a policy are categorically distinct from the reasons by which he publicly defends it. The two sets of reasons may overlap, or they may not, but in neither case need we conclude that politics is a cynical business. The reason lies in what we may call the *dimensions* of a political act. One such dimension concerns the practicality of the act in question. Will it have the desirable effects expected of it? What are its costs, and possible longer-term consequences? For the government to guarantee everyone an old-age pension, for example, will certainly alleviate hardship, but it will also have economic consequences because the incentives to thrift and saving will diminish, and that will affect the economy. The real test is the long term. As the nineteenth-century journalist Walter Bagehot observed, one cannot judge the consequences of any reform until the generation in which it was passed has left the scene.

A second dimension: what is the consequence of pursuing this particular *type* of policy? It will infallibly become a precedent used in arguing for further policies of the same type. If it fails, there may be demands that the policy be pursued even further, rather than abandoned. When central direction of some economic activity produces anomalies, for example, the typical demand is that further central direction should be invoked to deal with the anomalies. Another dimension: what effect will this policy have on the short- and long-term prospects of its promoter? The promoter here is both the individual and the party legislating the policy. The Welfare State, for example, created in Britain after 1945, diffused benefits widely over the electorate, and its short-term effects might therefore have been to increase support for the Labour Party which carried it out. In the event, this did not happen – Labour lost the 1951 election. More seriously still, some welfare measures of the period have been thought to have 'gentrified' the working class and detached them from the Labour Party. As politicians sometimes say, nothing fails like success.

A typical form of cynicism revolves around concepts such as the 'public interest' or the 'common good'. It is easy to discredit such terms by pointing out that nearly every act of government will have both good and bad consequences for different sets of people. But it is to mistake the meaning of public interest to think it can be judged in terms of individual costs and benefits. Ideas of this kind are formal terms of political argument whose specific meaning can only emerge from the public debate itself. They are the necessary formal conditions of any political advocacy. It would be absurd for a politician to say: 'I want to do this because it is good for *me*.' Such a line would provide no reason why anyone else should do it. No doubt there is a vague sense in which everything any politician advocates is the best thing for him in the circumstances, but this does not at all mean that he is a hypocrite out for nothing else but personal benefit. There is plenty of self-serving conduct in politics, though it is reasonable to think that politicians are generally more rather than less public-spirited than the rest of us. That may not be much, of course, but it is something.

None of this is to deny the lowness of much of politics. A certain craftiness is essential. To know, for example, the rule whereby when votes are equal in a committee, the motion is lost, tells the crafty politician whether to frame a precarious motion in negative or in positive terms. For if, opposing the policy, he frames it in positive terms, and the vote is tied, then the motion is lost and he gets what he wants. In the 1994 Euro-elections in Britain, one candidate got thousands of votes from an unsophisticated electorate by calling himself the 'literal' (rather than liberal) democratic candidate. To have a name beginning with the early letters of the alphabet gives a candidate a slight but measurable advantage from the dimness of some citizens who simply fill in the ballot-paper from the top down. And no one called 'Kennedy' can fail to pick up extra votes in many American states. The main delinquencies of politicians, however, arise from highly prevalent human vices: cowardice in failing to challenge the fashionable opinion which the politician senses is wrong, fear of being thought stupid, desire to take up a virtuous-seeming posture, a preference for the comfortable option when the politician knows that the chickens will come home to roost some time after he has left the scene, and so on.

Politicians form a kind of club, sharing a culture in liberal democracies which cuts across party divisions. Friendships, for example, are often warmer *across* parties than within them. Certain ideas are always dominant in this culture, and some of these ideas may run counter to the opinions (known here as prejudices) of the people at large. In recent times, capital punishment, multiculturalism, and international idealism are examples of this class of idea, and politicians sometimes confuse them with the quite different thing called principle. The significance of this fact is that in certain respects politicians as a class constitute an oligarchy whose tendency is at odds with that of the population it rules. This oligarchic tendency is even more pronounced in countries whose electoral system requires voters to support party lists. When the gap between what politicians admire and what the people want widens, the general stock of politicians goes down, and they are recognized less as representing than as trying to hoodwink the people. The familiar ambiguities of politics become explicit sophistry. This is, of course, a dangerous situation in which opportunities for demagogues multiply.

The politician facing the question: how may my policy be commended to my audience? will think more of his audience than of his own introspections. Sometimes that audience will be colleagues, sometimes his own party, and sometimes the electorate as a whole. We may assume that he is persuaded of its wisdom, but the reasons which seem decisive to him may well not be decisive to others. The problem of persuasion is to find the reasons that will be decisive to the audience. In doing that, the politician must take off from whatever common ground he shares with them. The first act in persuasion is for the persuader to convince his audience of his fellow-feeling with their broad aims, and only then can he commend his own policy as something fitting in with those aims.

What this account of persuasion suggests is that the politician must be a special type of person, one capable of keeping his deepest convictions to himself. The rest of us can shoot off our mouths to our hearts' content, indulging in that massive new pleasure the modern world has invented, being opinionated about matters on which we are ignorant. The politician must generally consider the effect of his opinions on his likely future, and requires a special kind of personality structure. But it should not be concluded from this that a politician is simply a hypocrite. Such a person is engaged in a high-risk occupation in which he must always be looking to future developments. Opportunism is certainly part of the talent, but unless the politician has genuine convictions – both moral convictions, and convictions about how things are likely to move – he will lack the clear profile which is usually necessary for the greatest success. Statesmen – the highest grade of politician – are those who can balance inner conviction with the talent of turning every opportunity to advantage. Charles de Gaulle called for resistance to Germany from London in 1940, and withdrew from French politics in 1946, taking risks in both cases which could have doomed him to obloquy and insignificance. Churchill's stand against appeasement in the 1930s might have been a mere swansong to a moderately successful career. A Barry Goldwater who took disastrous risks in bidding for the presidency in 1964 turned out to be preparing the soil for the Reagan victory of 1980. The secret of politics is to care about success, but not too much.

Chapter 9
The Experience of Politics:
II. Parties and Doctrines

Participating in liberal democratic politics means joining or supporting a political party. It means taking sides about some central political issues. W. S. Gilbert got it bang to rights when he wrote in *Iolanthe*:

> I often think it's comical
> How nature always does contrive
> That every boy and every gal
> That's born into the world alive
> Is either a little Liberal,
> Or else a little Conservative!

Gilbert was talking about nineteenth-century Britain, of course; in other countries the names and the emphases would be different. American Democrats and Republicans are perhaps not as distinct personalities as Liberal and Conservative, and twentieth-century Britain would require attention to the Labour Party. Further, we must remember that the actual names of political parties are opportunistic: mere names, not descriptions of doctrine. Republicans are no less democratic than Democrats, and Democrats just as republican. But Gilbert was right in thinking that in modern politics liberal and conservative tendencies are basic, and also that everything tends to reduce to two.

Certainly not one. Political scientists long accepted the terminology of 'the one-party state', but only because they were confused. The very word 'party' implies that there must be another party of the same basic kind. The essence of politics is debate, and there must be something to debate *with*. A party that monopolizes power and talks only to itself, like the ruling communist parties of the twentieth century, can only be totalitarian, which is to say despotic, and therefore quite distinct from politics. In every liberal democratic state, then, there will generally be two dominant parties, with several others on the margins of political power, not to mention a host of political sects which sometimes compete at elections. This sketch of the opinionative reality of a modern state needs to be completed by recognizing that parties are closely connected with a miscellany of pressure-groups, interest groups, vocational organizations, public relations firms, lobbyists, churches, and any other body which from time to time feels the need to influence the decisions of an increasingly ubiquitous state.

Parties seek to win elections, but this does not quite mean to 'capture the power of the state'. Indeed, it happens just as much that the state captures *them*. Policies that sound impressive in electoral rhetoric can turn out to be invitations to disaster once the incoming ministers discover their implications. The experience of government tends to mitigate the noisy contrasts of political debate, for government is a limited and responsible business while democratic politics is a game in which teams vie for victory. Risks must be taken, there are winners and losers, favoured candidates lose the race to rivals whom no one had taken seriously before, and all this constitutes a spectacle which inspires and enlivens partisans. As Edmund Burke expressed the benefits of competition in politics: 'He that wrestles with us strengthens our nerves and sharpens our skill. Our antagonist is our helper.' The basic constitutional point is that the electorate can 'throw the rascals out'.

Gilbert thought that political partisanship was innate, and there may indeed be some universal disposition which supports political tendencies. The American philosopher William James suggested that human beings are either tough-minded or tender-minded, and some have thought socialists, with their talk of compassion, to be tender-minded, while conservatives, who these days tend to support the free market, are tough-minded. This is not a view which will long survive a close inspection of contemporary political leaders.

Sometimes the complexity of parties is identified with the abstract issue of promoting or resisting change. Changes may, of course, be good or bad according to judgement, but conservatives have a generalized disposition to dislike change as such, while liberals welcome it. This distinction in turn is sometimes given a biological basis: the young are eager for change, but grow more conservative as they age. Certainly it is true that the young are significantly different in politics, being given to investing their boundless enthusiasm in ideas of social transformation – as did the Young Turks, the Bolsheviks, Mussolini's Fascists, Hitler's Nazis, and the youthful enthusiasts of the 1960s. This is not, on the face of it, a reason for encouraging the political engagement of the young!

Alternatively, parties may be identified with interests, so that the rich are conservative while the poor are liberal or socialist. The modern version of this classical understanding of politics derives from the Marxist idea that modern states are the arenas of a concealed war between the bourgeoisie and the proletariat. The idea suffers from two major disadvantages. The first is that in a war, one side seeks the total defeat of the other, whereas political debate, being a form of sport, is a type of competition in which each side *needs* the other. Just as you cannot play football without a competing team, so you cannot engage in politics without competing parties. The idea of the class war is therefore a covert way of recommending an end to politics and its replacement by leaders who will bring about the one true community. The second disadvantage of the idea that political parties merely reflect interests is that very significant numbers of workers vote for conservative parties while many rich and middle-class people espouse radical programmes, including the redistribution of wealth in the name of equality. Political scientists who start off with this idea have spent a lot of fruitless time scratching their heads over such phenomena as the blue-collar Republican or the Tory working man. The reality is that politics is about persuasion, and no brute fact about voters reliably tells us how they will think or act.

These ideas all help to illuminate aspects of a complex and shifting scene, and they mitigate what is the most plausible error in the understanding of parties: namely, to identify them with doctrines, sometimes called ideologies. Principles and programmes are important in politics, but both are trumped by circumstance. The problem is that circumstances are so infinitely various that the student of politics is forced to attend to doctrines which at least have some degree of intellectual coherence. In many cases, doctrine is almost the only guide we have as to how policy is moving; in any case, it has an intellectual attraction of its own which makes it worth study, however clear one must always be about its limited role in the actual exercise of authority.

The reader will have noticed that we have so far recognized liberalism and conservatism, but given only glancing mention to socialism, in some respects the official doctrine of left-wing parties in modern politics. In disentangling this area, only the most delicate footwork will do, and part of the argument will be incomplete until we deal with ideologies in a later chapter. Let us deal with the matter narratively, and base ourselves on British experience, which has been widely copied.

While division into party or faction has always been found in politics, and Cavalier fought Roundhead in the middle of the seventeenth century, the first recognizable political parties in England were the Whigs and Tories, who distinguished each other as enemies in 1679 over the bill to exclude James, Duke of York, from the throne because he was a Roman Catholic. Tories tended to believe in order and obedience, while Whigs, an aristocratic faction, based politics on the consent of a limited electorate as expressed in the institution of Parliament. Success in English politics over the next century nevertheless still depended largely on royal favour, and it was long before parties became respectable, and the institution of an opposition an integral part of the constitution.

The philosopher of the Whigs was John Locke, whose doctrines that government must rest on the consent of the governed, and that men have a natural right to life, liberty, and property are the basis of one version of liberalism. They were brilliantly echoed in the American Declaration of Independence of 1776, which talks of the inalienable right to 'life, liberty and the pursuit of happiness'. Here, then, was a doctrine which challenged the inherited traditional ways, and appealed to the disposition to reform both politics and society. The claim to be free from whatever restraints cannot meet the test of reason may plausibly be seen as the claim which has built the modern world, and for this reason the term 'liberalism' has acquired two meanings: first, as a specific political tendency in modern politics to be contrasted with conservatism and other doctrines; and second, as the archetypical attitude to which *all* modern European politics belongs.

The actual name liberalism only came into currency in the 1830s, the decade of political naming, in which socialism and conservatism also acquired their present names. But already by this time British politics had bifurcated in response to the defining event of modern politics. That grand question was how to understand what began to happen in France in 1789. Charles James Fox, one of the leading Whigs, believed that the French were at last following the path England had taken back in 1688; his friend Edmund Burke thought that the French revolutionaries, deriving their destructive policies from the abstract principles of the Declaration of the Rights of Man, were a new and thoroughly bad phenomenon. They were abandoning tradition in order to subject France (and soon Europe) to the brutalities of an abstract blueprint which must, Burke believed, destroy humanity. Burke's response to the French Revolution anticipated all the arguments used in the West against communism. Both the French and the Russian version of utopianism ended by drenching their countries in blood. Burke had predicted that this would happen in France long before the first head rolled off the guillotine.

Burke in effect founded conservatism by his diagnosis that liberalism as a political doctrine of reform found it hard to distinguish itself from doctrines of social transformation which, in their vain and destructive search for a perfect society, would destroy politics altogether. The basic arguments are brilliantly laid out in his *Reflections on the Revolution in France* (1790). What further entangled the understanding of politics with the confusions of despotism was the currency of the distinction between left and right. Originating as a metaphor based on the seating of factions in the French revolutionary assembly, left and right came to stand for revolution and reaction, two concepts which Burke and other exponents of politics would regard as equally unpolitical. According to Burke, politics is based, rather, on the concepts of preservation and reform, and it takes off not from abstract ideas of social perfection, but from the circumstances of the present.

What, then, of socialism? It arises from the fusion of two nineteenth-century phenomena: first, the idea that society is basically a factory whose products ought to be equally distributed among those who work in it, and second, the actual enfranchisement of the new class of industrial workers in the course of the century. Socialism finds its distinctiveness in its concern for the poor, and it seeks to legislate policies such as the redistribution of wealth and state provision of welfare which will equalize conditions of life. It is hostile to luxury and the idleness of the rich.

What is it that distinguishes socialism from liberalism and conservatism? As a doctrine of reform in a modern society, socialism would seem to have more in common with liberalism's bent for reform, and indeed in Britain the Labour Party rose under liberalism's wing and eventually replaced the Liberal Party as the self-declared party of reform. On the other hand, it was the Conservative Shaftesbury who introduced the Factory Acts in the 1840s, and conservative governments which after 1951 continued and extended Labour's Welfare State. When in 1985 British coal-miners went on strike against a Conservative government which wanted to make the mines economically efficient, the Labour Party had been supporting an essentially conservative policy of subsidy in order to preserve the mining villages.

This is a common situation. Parties steal each other's clothes and poach each other's supporters as part of the great game of politics, often with relatively little concern for doctrinal consistency. Liberals who used to stand for free trade became defenders of subsidy and protection with the so-called New Liberalism of the 1890s. Margaret Thatcher's Conservative government after 1979 was accused of betraying conservatism and espousing classical liberalism. Circumstances so change the colour of politics that what looks to a party like the right policy in some circumstances may look completely different a generation later. One of the most fascinating facts of modern politics is the failure of a successful socialist party to emerge in the United States. The Democratic Party has, of course, adopted many of the policies that would be called 'socialist' in Europe, and 'liberal' as an American political term means something far closer to socialism than its European counterpart. For almost any justification of policies will be abstract, and in new circumstances, will commit a party to more than it really wants. When that happens, policy or doctrine (and sometimes both) will have to be adjusted.

In actual politics, the formula that liberals, broadly, favour reform, and conservatives stick with tradition, points us in the right direction, but no more. In any case, it leaves us with the problem of socialism. Is socialism a tendency no less profoundly entrenched in politics than liberalism and conservatism? Or is it a movement which, transcending the ups and downs of political life, aims at something much grander than politics: a permanently better society? The basic point, we may suggest, is that socialism may refer either to belief in a fully just society, or to a political tendency to favour egalitarian and redistributive reforms when possible. Whatever it might be like, a fully just society would need no serious politics; it would be one of those projects of perfection which we shall call ideologies and which we shall discuss presently. And this is what the term socialism commonly signifies, especially to its adherents. That is why it has acquired a genuinely political partner, often called social democracy, where the addition of democracy signifies the political commitment which recognizes that the state is an institution that must respond to the current tastes and desires of its members, and therefore that any conception of a finally perfect state is incompatible with the very activity of politics itself.

Chapter 10

The Experience of Politics: III. Justice, Freedom, and Democracy

Politics, being largely talk, must dramatize itself. A king is in some sense just one human being among others. Civil order in a monarchy requires that we *dramatize* what it is to be a king, and this is the point of crowns, thrones, sceptres, guards of honour, regalia, and other symbols, some of which are used by the prime ministers and presidents of our own egalitarian times. Most political expression is metaphorical. The state, we saw, was a *body* politic. We may now consider it as a ship. The ship metaphor lies behind the very word 'government' which comes from the medieval Latin *gubernaculum*, a rudder. Politics is the art of navigating the ship of state. By what signs should the steersman steer?

The obvious answer is: he should be guided by *ideals*, distant beacons of excellence at which we should all aim. Ideals are often the concepts by which political parties identify themselves. Conservatives, for example, owe a general allegiance to tradition, liberals to freedom, socialists to equality. But the supreme navigational tool of politics, trumping even these, is the thing called 'justice' which in the first masterpiece of political philosophy, Plato's *Republic*, was the regulative virtue which determined the place of all the other virtues. The actual word justice comes from the Latin *ius*, which covers both law and right. In his famous dialogue, Plato began by showing that justice meant giving every person his due, but went on to demonstrate that this formula meant nothing until one could explain what was due (or owing) to people. This required nothing less than sketching the entire structure of a *polis*. It turned out that justice on Plato's view was fitting people into the place in the state for which their natures equipped them. Rulers were thus revealed as philosophers, for only philosophers possessed a rational understanding of human nature. The basic principle was complementarity. Workers, warriors, and philosopher-rulers must each stick to their own tasks.

Plato's republic is sometimes taken to be a utopia, that is, a picture of some ideal condition, but this is a mistake. For one thing, desires differ, and there is no reason why I should find your desires admirable, or you mine. What is merely desired has no intellectual force, whereas what is *desirable* moves the argument on to an objective plane beyond desire. More profoundly, however, justice is an ideal, and nothing in the complex real world in which we live can actually *be* an ideal. In navigational terms, justice is a star to steer by, and when you steer by a star you don't aim to arrive there. This point is sometimes made by saying that justice is a normative concept, which means that we ought to take our bearings from it. To say that justice requires a certain policy, or that some existing situation is unjust, is to propose action. When we talk about justice, then, we might be describing an ideal, sketching a utopia, stating a grievance, or advancing some policy, or indeed doing a variety of other things. The essential thing about justice and other ideals is that they function in many different ways, and it is important always to ask in any particular case which function is being performed.

Is it just, for example, that the right to vote should be limited to people with property, or to adult males? Is it just that one nation should be ruled by another? Is it just that the state's religion should be enforced on everyone? These questions have been passionately debated in terms of justice, and different answers have been given in different generations. It is obvious, then, that the content of justice will at least to some extent depend on current opinion. It happens that most people will have a clear answer to each of the questions I have used in illustration, and will therefore be tempted to think that human beings move steadily from narrower to broader and more defensible ideas of justice as time goes by. This is one of our most satisfying illusions. All that experience actually seems to demonstrate is that each generation is pleased to discern that it has at last arrived at decently absolute moral and political judgements.

However democratic a state's constitution may be, for example, the participation of its citizens goes up and down according to nothing more profound than circumstances. The citizens of Classical times participated in politics more than those in the Middle Ages; and the citizens of Italian cities early in the Middle Ages more than those in the later period. Things swing back and forth. Recent generations have tended to make an absolute out of the belief that moral standards are relative and all cultures are equal, fondly imagining that this, at last, is the wisdom of the ages.

Politics is endless public disagreement about what justice requires. Aristotle taught that instability in constitutions is caused by the passion for equality, and went on to characterize justice as a state in which honour and office are distributed according to the contribution different groups make to the welfare of the *polis*. Numbers, wealth, and merit must all find a place, and a true polity would include both democratic and oligarchic elements. Here the philosopher is merely telling us what justice is. He is not giving advice on how to achieve it, and his formula would hardly be of much use if he were. And that reveals to us yet another way in which an idea like justice can function: it can supply a philosophical explanation of what we already know. For there is one great defect of the navigational metaphor we have been using: it suggests that justice is to be found in some place we have not yet reached. This is quite wrong. We already know what justice is, and our societies already are, in certain basic ways, just. If this were not so, we could not recognize it. Justice is, in other words, not merely something ahead of us and useful in navigating; it is also something behind us which tells us both what we are and where we have come from.

That is why political life is full of people demanding justice on some point or other. With new ideas or changed circumstances, conditions which previously seemed natural come to provoke demands for reform, and justice is the formula for demanding reform. In that rhetorical role, the term can be cheapened and trivialized. Available to everybody with a demand or a grievance, it can focus passions which lead to a descent into civil disorder. Whole societies can collapse into civil war because two sides whistle up the idea of justice to support their contentions. It happened in the United States in 1860, and Hobbes thought it caused the English civil war. He therefore followed another philosophical tradition, which plays down justice as the basis of order and insists that the real issue is peace. Assigning the absolute responsibility for deciding what is just to the sovereign, Hobbes described the just man, with brutal formality, as '*he that in his actions observeth the laws of his country*', thus denying the validity of people consulting their consciences in order to discover some higher justice in conflict with current public policy. It is not that philosophers such as Hobbes did not care about justice, or conscience. 'What are kingdoms without justice, but great robberies?' asked St Augustine, for whom earthly justice could be nothing better than a pale imitation of heaven. It was simply that they thought of justice as inflammable material ignitable by the sparks of passion, and therefore best kept under philosophical lock and key.

The way in which ideals function in political talk may be illustrated by the ideal which we may call indifferently either *liberty*, after the Roman god Liber, a version of Dionysus, or *freedom* after the Germanic term meaning those, dear to the head of the household, who were not slaves. Freedom functions above all as a term of self-identification: identifying, for example, classes of people who do not have a master, and sometimes republican constitutions without monarchical authority. Its broadest meaning distinguishes those ruled politically from those ruled despotically, and it was this meaning to which the West appealed in calling itself 'the free world' as against the despotic rule of communist parties in Russia and elsewhere. Here, then, we have an ideal term towards which we do not need to navigate because (as with justice) we have it already. Our task, rather, is to keep in good repair what we already have.

The most obvious way to construe freedom is negatively: it means not being restrained. In political contexts, this means not having to live one's life under a ruler who has arbitrary powers. It is an easy sophism, however, to argue that if freedom means not being restrained, and if I am, as it were, restrained from doing what I want by lack of money, then poverty is unfreedom. In this way, the term 'freedom' can slip into 'power' and we are well launched on the road towards positing some benign despot who will abolish poverty and equalize our power. Again, Hobbes was no less suspicious of freedom than he was of justice, and he defined it very carefully as 'the silence of the law'. One was free, that is to say, where no constraining legal rule obliged one to conform. The more familiar European tradition, however, has been to define freedom as the condition of living under the rule of law, by contrast with subjection to arbitrary command. Yet even this sensible view conceals possible problems. If freedom is nothing else but the absence of restraint, then how can we be free at the point where a law restrains us from doing what we want? This was the view taken by Hobbes, and his follower Jeremy Bentham, but the point at issue requires us to realize that a law (by contrast with a command) is purely abstract and leaves the discretion unfettered. Most people, for example, are not powerfully constrained by sanctions against solving one's problems by murder. They grow up instinctively excluding it as an acceptable option.

As they cruise life's boundless and bottomless sea, the passengers on the ship of a particular state might well decide that they want to steam towards something they do not yet enjoy, or enjoy but imperfectly. Such a decision assumes that all can enjoy the ideals that attract them.

This is a profound mistake. The reality is that our character and our culture at a given time limit what is possible for us; only certain sorts of people can enjoy certain sorts of ideals. Criminals, for example, are not very good at justice, though they often have remarkable capacities for honour. Again, the Western ideal of freedom is irresistibly attractive to many in other civilizations, but depends on forms of self-control which are not easily acquired. Reckless and visionary theorists have persuaded many to discern a destination adjacent to freedom called 'liberation' and it has induced excitable passengers on leaky ships of state to agree to violent changes of direction. Some have foundered, and not surprisingly, because as Rousseau and others have pointed out, when slaves revolt, they will not create a free society, but merely change their masters. The paradox of freedom is the fact that it can *only* be a possession we already have. As an ideal to navigate by, it must always be an illusion.

The ideal of democracy has many features similar to that of liberty. Beginning life as a humble constitutional term, it has grown so big that it threatens to take over the territories of both freedom and justice. It is easy to illustrate the simpler ways in which democracy might do this: no one can be free, Rousseau argued, who does not participate in making the laws under which he lives. Rousseau himself was too sensitive a philosopher to move directly from this proposition to the idea that only democracies are free (he thought democracy a constitution requiring gods to work it), but many others have. There are many ways in which democracy might digest justice, though the idea that only democracies are just would have the implausible implication that all but a tiny handful of societies in history have been unjust.

Democracy supremely illustrates the way in which political ideals have in the modern world expanded beyond the arena of the state and been set up as criteria of value in those other associations which (as we saw in Chapter 6) constitute modern life. A democratic *society*, for example, might be thought a contradiction in terms, but has come to mean a society in which everyone leads the same kind of life and disposes of similar resources. A democratic *culture* is one liberated from élitist standards of what constitutes beauty. Sometimes there is even talk of democratizing the *economy*, which generally means turning factories into worker cooperatives. Even manners can be democratic, and democracy was the term the French historian Alexis de Tocqueville used to describe the American society which he thought would supersede the aristocratic customs of Europe.

The societies in which Westerners currently live are all in basic ways just, free, and democratic. These terms, when elaborated by philosophers, plausibly describe our philosophical foundations. But each of these terms can be refined by philosophers and rhetoricians (each in a different way) so as to shimmer before us not as customs and conditions we already enjoy, but as new directions we might take. They turn into social justice, liberation, and real or strong democracy, and guide our strivings. One type of politics is, then, navigation by ideals. The problem is, of course, that you can only steer by one star, not by several scattered over the heavens. That means that those who promote the claims of one star rather than another must show that it is the one star which will lead to the satisfaction of *all* our strivings. But since many of our strivings are mutually contradictory, we must give up either some of our strivings or some of these destinations. And that is why the direction of politics must always be an outcome of changing judgements about conflicting desirabilities. Ideals are important in politics, but in the end realities must determine where we go, and how fast we travel.

Chapter 11
Studying Politics Scientifically

The idea that governing a state is like steering a ship is so marvellously seductive that it dominates modern politics. The metaphor has spread into discussions of purposes, policies, strategies, programmes, and other bits of terminology suggesting that there is a 'we' that can determine the future of vast and complex societies. Parties at election times compete for votes with promises of benefits, while experience shows that problems are solved, if solved they ever are, only at the cost of creating new ones. This is, no doubt, the human condition, but within that condition we may perhaps have a limited choice between facing our problems as individuals or as collectivities. Some dream of political salvation from the injustices we suffer, while many would echo Alexander Pope's statement of the opposite position:

> For forms of government let fools contest.
> Whate'er is best administered, is best.

If governing a state is like steering a ship, however, what we need are reliable facts and sound explanations of how the vessel works. The place to find these, it is widely believed, is in science. So far we have looked at the history of politics, and we then turned our attention to the ways in which it is experienced. Let us now move from history and practice to science.

The important thing to realize is that seeing politics scientifically requires a complete change of perspective. The way we experience politics is as a drama of character, convention, and circumstance. Political science requires that we forget about individual differences and construe politics, over time, as a *process*, analogous to what happens in nature. We have seen that the ancients did this by detecting cross-generational cycles in the movement of politics, a powerful idea even today, and one used to great effect by Machiavelli. Religion, he remarked, 'brought forth good institutions and good institutions led to good fortune, and from good fortune came the felicitous success of the city's undertakings'. He followed Polybius and other ancient writers in arguing that each constitution collapsed from its inherent defects. Such cycles are only marginally affected by the individual qualities of those involved. He does note, however, that many such cycles never complete themselves because weakness, caused by disorder in a state, makes it prey to conquest by neighbours who are outside the system within which the cycle is working itself out.

The idea of a system, that is, a set of mechanical components having a fixed relation to each other, is central to conceiving of politics scientifically. A car engine is an example of such a system: when a car breaks down, a mechanic may be able to fix it. We often think of an economy as a piece of machinery whose outcomes an outside intelligence, such as a government, can direct, rather as if the government were the owner of a car and wanted to enhance its performance, or increase its gearing. Here, then, we have another of those dominant metaphors by which politics is understood: not a body this time, nor a ship, but a mechanism. The politician is an engineer, a mechanic outside the system, trying to make the machinery work the way we want. We must distinguish, too, between what is internal to the system (which in current technical language is called 'endogenous') and what influences it from outside (which is similarly called 'exogenous').

This metaphor underlies political science. The science element consists in the attempt to understand politics as a process or mechanism, and closely related is a technological ambition to use such knowledge to achieve our ends. One difficulty in conceiving of politics in this way is deciding on the boundaries between the endogenous and the exogenous. Where, in other words, does the system end and the outside manipulative intelligence begin? When Charles de Gaulle intervened in French politics in 1958, for example, and set up a whole new constitution (or system) in the form of the Fifth Republic, was he a *deus ex machina* outside the system, or was he part of the wider system constituted by the tradition of French politics? The answer is, of course, that it all depends on the rules of the intellectual game of understanding being played. The American Founding Fathers can be regarded as setting up a system of rules within which their successors have operated.

When we deliberate about something, we assume ourselves to be free and outside any system, but when other people deliberate about us, they take us as having fixed and more or less predictable characteristics within a system of understanding. It is a current philosophical cliché to insist that no one can escape the determining system constituted by race, gender, class, history, or other abstractions, and in one sense this is obviously true. But it would only be an interesting truth if the system constituted by race, gender, class, and history could tell us just how people are going to act. Since it cannot, we are left with a vacuous determinism: we can't escape – whatever it is that we can't escape!

Political science rests, then, on a foundation best understood in terms of the metaphor of engineering. It also rests upon a rhetoric which contrasts image, stereotype, fiction, myth (and the term 'rhetoric' itself) with fact, evidence, reality, and other such hard, gritty, impressive terms. Building on these foundations, political science uses its materials to construct a grand edifice of theory – and, today, such materials! The political scientist first appears before us as the proprietor of a bottomless mine of data. Data is (the Latin plural has become a collective singular) the set of facts which can be used to construct and test theories: the whole of history can be melted down to provide one kind of data for the political scientist advancing a theory of, for example, revolutions. The modern world may almost be defined as a progressive intoxication with data. Civil servants collect it, statisticians refine it, and computers store it. The political scientist is in danger of becoming like those generals whose intelligence is so vast that the plan and timing of the enemy attack are known but unrecognized because so much other information is flooding headquarters.

A vote is a piece of data, and so is the answer to a pollster's question, and all over the world the volume of this kind of information is expanding exponentially. Votes and opinions only become data, however, if turned into abstractions constituted by the limited choice offered in the election, or the answer to the pollster's question. Data begins in homogenization, and must always in the end defeat the many ingenious attempts which are made to incorporate complexities, such as the degree of enthusiasm of the voter, or the qualifications of the respondent. It is not just that such complexities are not, in principle, capable of being turned into data; it is rather that the relevant information is not always consciously available to the respondent at the moment of response. Human beings are more than compositions of conclusions held with varying degrees of intensity.

Politics as the political scientist sees it is, then, systems thickened with data, and the aim is to find causal connections between them. In this search, the analysis of modern societies into distinct associations (which we studied in Chapter 6) is an invaluable framework of thought – but also one which threatens to destroy political science itself. For if the causes of what happens in politics are to be found in the economy, or social processes, or even culture, then politics is merely a set of effects, and loses its autonomy as a free and self-determining activity. One consequence would be that there is nothing in politics for a science to study.

89

Politics *is* in fact autonomous, though it is obviously closely related to other human activities and structures. The basic question in political science is: what causes such and such a political phenomenon? Why, for example, do governments sometimes win elections and sometimes lose them? It may be possible to find part of the answer to this question within politics itself: for example, in the superior party organization of the winner. But what often appeals to political scientists as a more profound explanation will be an explanation outside politics altogether – in, for example, the apparently separate thing called the economy. One simple hypothesis of this kind has been that governments get re-elected if the election is held on a rising curve of the trade cycle. If this were in fact true, it would illustrate the maxim that knowledge is power. All that a government need do to win an election is to engineer a boom as the election approaches.

The two obvious problems are, first, that the economy is not a domesticated pet which will do what it is told, and second, as it happens, that the hypothesis is in any case false. As is common in political science, the correlation is interesting but the causal nexus is feeble, even though the elements of the relationship – the consumer and the voter – are unified by being the same person.

There is a further problem which can be illustrated by one of the early projects of creating a political science in its modern form. At the turn of the twentieth century, the first wave of academic political scientists attacked some of their theoretical predecessors for the supposed mistake of assuming that human beings were entirely rational. This mistake had allegedly been made by politicians and theorists who had tried to appeal to voters in terms of purely rational argument. The new political scientists triumphantly pointed out that image, stereotype, the emotions arising in crowds, family background, and many other irrational factors were actually the main determinants of political behaviour. As often happens in such critical interactions in academic life, the two sides were to some extent at cross-purposes – the new political scientists taking for a factual assumption what was actually a normative argument designed to elicit more rational attitudes to political policy.

Even more fundamental than critic and criticized being at cross-purposes is the fact that the project of political science is limited by having to assume that human conduct is essentially non-rational. Science turns whatever it studies into a natural process which is not affected by thinking, because thought is the capacity to construe the world in a variety of ways, and how human beings act depends on these unpredictable constructions. Human conduct thus lacks even the regularity found in the natural world. The observation that governments often win elections which are held on a rising or high level of prosperity, for example, can be turned into something like the causal hypothesis that citizens, happy with this condition, tend to vote for the incumbent government. But it is because human beings are reflective, and the world can be seen in many other ways beside that of prosperity or its absence, that the hypothesis lacks real force.

There are, indeed, a variety of different forms of irrational human behaviour as it is studied by psychologists, and to this extent political science in the twentieth century has generated a vast number of fascinating hypotheses and helped to organize in interesting ways the information which is in fact indispensable to understanding the politics of any particular nation. But, in the behavioural form we have just been sketching, it has proved something of a disappointment, and fallen behind a new model of political science which tackles the problem from the other direction. Instead of concentrating on emotions and reflexes, rational choice theory concerns itself with rational deliberation. Politicians and voters are constantly making choices, and we choose in terms of our preferences as modified by our ideas about the probable course of events. This is called 'expected utility' and can be studied in terms of a formal logic of preference. A particular development of this study looks at the relations between separate decision-makers choosing 'strategies' in what are (misleadingly) called 'games'. The question asked by rational choice theorists is: under what conditions is it rational to choose a strategy of co-operation with others (paying for public goods, such as parks or defence, for example) as against what (on these assumptions) is the most immediately obvious rational strategy, that of pursuing one's individual advantage, and being a 'free rider' on what others have paid for?

These issues are often analysed on the basis of the famous prisoner's dilemma, in which two prisoners kept incommunicado by the sheriff must decide on their strategies. The conditions are that if A confesses and B does not, then A gets off with a light sentence and B a heavy one. If B confesses, it will be he who gets off lightly and A who will suffer. If they both confess, they will both get quite a heavy sentence. If, however, they trust each other, and neither confesses, both will get the lightest sentence of all. Trust is thus, in this game as in life, risky, but it can also have the greatest pay-off. It is remarkable how extensively this unlikely structure can be formalized to cover everything from the foundation of states to international relations and the provision of public spaces.

This axiomatics of choice has generated a large and impressive technical literature. What it illustrates is the propensity of political science to become colonized by economists, for the agents theorized in this way are basically economic actors. And it is this fact which explains what might well seem to the reader a contradiction in our argument. We have argued that political science can only understand human beings as irrational, mere responders to stimuli. Yet here in rational choice theory we have a form of political science which explores the choices of rational agents. Surely, then, political science can accommodate rationality?

The crux of this matter lies in what we mean by rational. We need not here go into the distinction between the concept of reason in classical philosophy on the one hand and the significantly different 'instrumental rationality' of abstract economic actors on the other. All we need to observe is that when human beings act, they seek *both* to realize the desires which impel the action, *and also* to express themselves in conserving a chosen identity. Rational choice theory can in a limited way turn the first element into a formula by quantifying and ordering preferences, but it cannot deal with the other element of action. And it is particularly the case in politics (and less so in economics) that this element of our conduct is especially prominent. Critics of rational choice theory have been especially savage in attacking its blindness to the way in which people of different cultures conduct themselves.

The scientific study of politics is, then, a great but limited achievement of our century. Like any other form of understanding, it gains its power from its limitations, but it happens that the specific limitations of science in its fullest sense are especially restrictive in the understanding of human life. But political science often escapes this limitation by ignoring the strict requirements of science as a discipline. Much of its material is historical and descriptive, as indeed it must be if we are to recognize that any understanding of the government of modern states cannot be separated from the culture of the people who live in them.

Chapter 12
Ideology Challenges Politics

Politics, along with physical labour and childbirth, is in Christian terms one of the curses of mankind. Machines have taken much of the sting from labour, and childbirth is no longer the pain it was. But what of the curse of politics? If men were angels, no government would be needed. But since some sort of government *is* needed, could we not find a better solution than the states revealed to us by history as riddled with war, poverty, and violence? High hopes of this kind have often erupted among the poor on the margins of politics, and have sometimes captured the centre. Such hopes unmistakably derive from a millennial version of Christianity, and they have had explosive consequences.

Anabaptists believing in the imminence of a new heavenly order took over the German town of Munster in 1534, for example, and instituted what was thought to be a perfect community. It bore a remarkable resemblance to modern totalitarianism. A tendency to religious despotism was evident in the English civil war after 1642. 'It is God's design', a clergyman wrote in typical vein, 'to bring forth the civil government, and all things here below, in the image and resemblance of things above.'

A powerful tradition with its roots in philosophy has also focused attention on the project of a perfect society. Many have been bewitched by Plato's account of the philosopher escaping the cave of shadows in which most people live and seeing the reality of things. The true ruler could only be the philosopher, for only philosophers had access to the knowledge needed to guide a true community. Much later, the eighteenth-century *philosophes* thought that their grasp of reason constituted the knowledge needed to bring justice to the world, a process many of them could not distinguish from sweeping away the *ancien régime*. It was these writers who abandoned the traditional Western loathing of despotism, for they recognized that the new order demanded not only knowledge but also unlimited power. The European state, largely bound by constitutionality and the rule of law, was for this very reason doomed to imperfection.

The modern soil in which these ideas has grown was prepared by Francis Bacon, who took the purpose of human life to be the accumulation of useful knowledge in the cause of improving human conditions. By the end of the eighteenth century, technology had acquired such power over nature that advanced thinkers were already dreaming of exercising the same sort of power over society. Their first adventure came in France in 1789. The fact that it culminated in blood and tyranny merely sent them back, as it were, to the drawing-board.

Many streams of thought fed an aspiration which resembled the search for magical power. Religious speculations about God's progressive revelation and the pantheist idea that God *is* the creation, rather than an external creator of it, spread into philosophy. In Scotland, a number of thinkers such as Adam Smith and Adam Ferguson saw the history of humanity as a progression of stages of evolution: people had evolved from nomads to a pastoral society which had given way to agriculture and culminated in the commercial society of modern times. Each step was taken to be a higher form of civilization, guided by what Adam Smith called the 'invisible hand'. In Germany, these and many other ideas came to be influentially expounded by the philosopher Hegel, who revealed to his readers that history, which sceptics saw merely as an up and down ride over the bumps of human folly, actually exhibited a rational structure. Hegel thought that history progressed; the subjects of a modern state enjoyed a fullness of experience which had merely been potential in earlier societies.

Hegel's was a formidable and complex philosophy, but it conveyed apocalyptic strivings to a group of young disciples who thought that he had solved, or at the very least nearly solved, the riddle of human existence. The most famous of them was Karl Marx, who fused Hegel with the burgeoning socialist ideas of early industrial Europe. Marx detected the fall of man in the institution of private property which had apparently emerged after the nomadic stage of primitive communism. The destiny of mankind was to recreate that early communal idyll in an advanced technological form, and that achievement it was which had necessitated the sufferings of history.

It was Marx's characterization of the modern world which gave him such influence. Hegel had argued that after the slaveries and oppressions of history, modern Europe had at last achieved a civilization in which all were free. Marx revealed to his followers that this formal freedom was actually the most subtle form of oppression ever created. Moderns were, on the view Marx and Engels sketched out in the *Communist Manifesto* of 1848, little more than puppets moved by the mysterious force of capital, which induced them to trade, migrate, work, and even think according to the concealed logic of the capitalist mode of production. There had been socialisms before, but Marx claimed that his was the first *scientific* socialism – the knowledge of the human condition which at last, after millennia of being buffeted by the waves of historical necessity, allowed mankind to seize the helm of the ship of state and guide it to port. It only required those who had this knowledge to seize the bridge in a process called revolution.

This was so brilliant a vulgarization of long-standing religious and philosophical themes that it has continued to fascinate subsequent generations. It combines a simple melodrama attractive to the people it was designed to mobilize – the unsophisticated proletariat – with an apparatus of ideas that could excite more intellectual followers. Hegel had been tempted to think that history had, in a sense, come to an end; Marx adopted the idea and located it in the future, as a project to be struggled for. Unlike Hegel, Marx consigned the state to what later Marxists called 'the dustbin of history'. Indeed, a great deal of what had hitherto constituted civilization would disappear in the new epoch: morality, for example, and law. Philosophy itself, that tortuous wrestling with complicated abstractions dating back to Thales and the Greek pre-Socratics, would be replaced by a direct, unmediated consciousness of human reality, available to all. As Marx wrote in one of his most famous utterances: 'The philosophers have only interpreted the world; the point is to change it.'

Marxism is important not only historically, but also because it served as a model for many later revelations of the same kind. Its devotees experienced the immense excitement of people for whom all the confusing elements of life had suddenly fallen into place. It was thus quite different from political writing. One might be a passionate liberal or conservative, support parliament or the king, advocate or oppose the extension of the franchise, and so on, without in any way imagining that these enthusiasms constituted a revelation. Indeed, in an age in which Christian belief was declining, Marxism was the economy package which supplied its followers with a politics, a religion, and a moral identity all in one. For this very reason, it is not a political doctrine, though if its claims were accepted, it would be something very much more significant. Political doctrines give reasons; they talk to each other. Marxism could only declare the truth. For Marx, politics is merely the froth cast up by deeper processes. We thus need to distinguish Marxism and similar revelations, on the one hand, from political doctrines, which have a quite distinct logic, on the other. We may call these doctrines, which promise an earthly liberation, ideologies, and our next task must be to explain this curious word.

It was invented in 1797 by a French philosopher called Destutt de Tracy who had recently survived the Terror by the skin of his teeth. Tracy was working on the central project of the *philosophes* of that period: to clarify the understanding by bringing concepts to the test of experience and discarding those that failed. He might have called this new science psychology, but thought that its derivation (from the Greek *psyche* meaning 'soul') might convey something unacceptably spiritual. So he invented 'ideology' and it caught on. Its proponents were soon called *idéologues*. As liberal republicans in the confused decade of the Revolution, they came to support a rising young officer called Bonaparte. He soon discarded them, referring contemptuously to *les idéologues* as theorists whose meddling in politics did more harm than good. Destutt de Tracy continued to develop his science of the understanding, over four volumes, up to 1815, but 'ideology' for the moment survived merely as an occasional term with which to express contempt for impractical intellectuals.

In 1846, Marx and Engels wrote a huge work called *The German Ideology* in which they attacked their former associates in the circle of young Hegelians. Possessing, as they believed, the truth about how society worked, they needed a term to describe the false beliefs of those (especially the bourgeoisie) who had failed to transcend their social situation. They took up the word 'ideology'. This work was not published until 1926, but the word was launched in a new direction. And already it will be clear that it contained two quite opposite ideas: that of truth and that of falsity. Ideology meant (for the ideologues themselves) a philosophical hygiene revealing truth, and (for Marx) the very falsity which needed to be cleansed. The problem of apparent contradiction disappears, however, when one realizes that the falsity of those false ideas is guaranteed by the truth of one's own ideas. Ideology refers, as it were, to the negative and positive poles of a dogmatic conviction. Marxists had a true understanding of the world, and therefore whatever contradicted them must be false – that is, ideological, which meant both false, and false *because* reflecting the wrong social location. The same ambivalent usage marks anarchist versions of the truth, or those of radical feminists. So long as one grasps this symbiosis, the term ideology can be used without serious confusion as referring *both* to the truth, and *also* to all the other beliefs which are judged to be false *in terms of that belief*. Ideology thus exhausts the entire field of truth and error, so long as one judges that one knows, as Marx and his followers thought they did, what the truth is.

We need to follow the adventures of this word a little further. The first adventure happened within Marxism itself. Marxism asserted that ideas reflected material conditions, and the false ideas of the bourgeoisie, reflecting bourgeois conditions, were 'bourgeois ideology'. But since all ideas were thought to be socially produced, the question must arise: where did communist ideas come from? The solution was that they bubbled up from the experience of the proletariat who were destined to bring truth-revealing communism into existence. Marxism in these terms was the ideology – the socially determined ideas – of the rising proletariat, which happened also to be true. Such is the view taken, for example, by Lenin, the most famous Marxist of his generation.

A second development resulted from the growth of political science as an academic discipline, especially in the United States, towards the end of the nineteenth century. Among the materials on offer for study were the rather miscellaneous theories of all those who had written, in one idiom or another, about politics. Words like 'theory' and 'doctrine' lacked the requisite technical panache for a developing inquiry, so 'ideology' came to be used to refer to this entire miscellany of beliefs, including both political ideas and what we are here marking off as a special kind of intellectual creation. 'Ideology' was foreign, and impressive-sounding, and was to generate many books with chapters recounting the arguments of the various 'isms' of which political debate is composed.

The story of the word is, then, remarkable, covering as it does the true, the false, and the political. Since a whole academic industry has grown up around the project of construing the very many variant meanings of this term, there is a clear case for leaving it to the mercies of nomenclatural mysticism. But its continuity with the past suggests that it remains useful. Ideologies, by contrast with political doctrines, claim exclusive truth. They explain not only the world, but the false beliefs of opponents as well. Ideologists possess the long-sought knowledge of how to abolish politics and create the perfect society. How might one put such a claim to the test? Marx himself wrote in the *Theses on Feuerbach* of 1846 that theoretical problems find their solution in practice. The logical character of Marxism, as of other ideologies, is by this test revealed in the actions of its followers when they come to power. What they have invariably done is to institute a reign of truth, in which discussion disappears and nothing else but the ideology is taught in schools, universities, the media, the law courts, and everywhere else. And this characterstic of Marxism is a universal truth, unaffected by culture. In Cuba among the Spanish Americans, in many states in Africa, in China, and most notably in the Soviet Union until its collapse, exactly the same policy was adopted, for it follows directly from the ideology itself.

It is easy to confuse ideologies and political doctrines, because how they look is always in large part determined (as with all rhetorical exercises) by audience and context. Communists and other ideologists operating in liberal democratic states must present their beliefs *as if* they were merely policy options to be supported by general and arguable reasons, for ideological dogmatism merely looks absurd except in conversation with fellow believers. On the other hand, enthusiasm may infect *any* political doctrine with the belief that its principles alone can save the world from evil. Libertarians who believe that political problems are caused only by governments interfering in the natural contractual relations between individuals are moving from a rhetorical to an ideological logic. 'Democracy' is sometimes the watchword of those who think that all political problems could be solved if only we became (what we are not yet) a *real* democracy. We may say that the constitutive illusion of ideology is that there is a possible structure of society whose achievement would allow rational actors to create a happy world.

Ideology is commonly signalled by the presence of a tripartite structure of theory. The first stage reveals to us that the past is the history of the *oppression* of some abstract class of person. It is concerned with workers as a class, not (as a politician might be) with workers at a particular time and place; or with women in general, or with this or that race. Specific discontents are all swept up into the symptomatology of the structurally determined oppression. The duty of the present is thus to mobilize the oppressed class in the *struggle* against the oppressive system. This struggle is not confined to the conventional areas of politics. It flares up everywhere, even in the remoter recesses of the mind. And the aim of this struggle is to attain a fully just society, a process generally called *liberation*. Ideology is thus a variation played on the triple theme of oppression, struggle, and liberation.

Politics, by contrast, assumes that any state will contain many ways of life, and that a responsive political order must make it possible for its subjects to follow their own bent. One implication of this practice is that most of life will *not* be about politics, any more than most of football consists of arguing with the referee. The doctrine that *everything* is political is an infallible sign of the ideological project of replacing the rule of law by the management of people. A further implication is that society will necessarily be imperfect, for if it allows people to be morally responsible, some of them are certainly going to be irresponsible.

Ideology challenges politics in the name of an ideal in which all desires are satisfied, but it first simplifies the issue by ruling out of court all but a remarkably limited schedule of approved desires, usually called 'needs'. The word 'community' often stands for a simple way of life which we all live in a single basic role, as comrade, sister, hedonist, or mere human being. The classic ideologists of the last two centuries dreamed of the drama of revolution. Their only conception of political activity was working to make this grand event come about. No moth ever flew into the flames with more enthusiasm than the revolutionary. Revolutions have turned out to be what drug users called 'a bad trip', but the dream from which the drama emerged is far from dead. We must next consider how it mingles with deeper currents of contemporary thought.

Chapter 13
Can Politics Survive the Twenty-first Century?

Machiavelli recounts in Book III of the *Discourses on the First Ten Books of Livy* the story of a rich Roman who gave food to the starving poor during a famine, and the Romans executed him for it. They reasoned that he was building up a following in order to become a tyrant. This response highlights the tension between morals and politics, and shows that the Romans cared more for freedom than for welfare. It throws into relief the fact that the way we judge actions depends on our idea of what politics is. Junius Brutus, who liberated the Romans from the tyrannical Tarquins, later executed his own sons for conspiring against the new regime. Does this show that politics is a dirty business, or that it calls on the most heroic dispositions possible to human beings? Certainly these Romans cannot be fitted into the modern view that politics is merely a service industry allowing us to get on with the game of life, or that rulers must create a perfectly just society.

Modern politicians and civil servants augment their power by giving food to the starving and the needy, but we do not execute them for it. Does this mean that we do *not* care for freedom? I do not think so, but the contrast between us and the Romans does raise some sharp questions. They are questions which bear upon the future of politics itself, and speculating about the way things are going is a major element of political thought. There is no junction in politics more important than that between present and future. Let us consider, then, as a model of this kind of argument, the issue of morality and politics. It may be put this way: philanthropy, charity, altruism, and helping the poor are perhaps morally admirable. What is their political significance?

Our question becomes even more penetrating if we remember that politics was born out of certain historical conditions, and might well die in the same way. It might die because something new and better is being born; or possibly because something very old and resilient is taking a new form. But if the activity of politics *were* to die, the institution of the state would go with it. To attack the one is to threaten the other. We have already discussed the ideological challenge which attacks the state in the name of a perfectly just society, where 'society' is a key term, partly because its real character is conveniently vague, and partly because society can stand (as the state cannot) for a *single* system of life. This single system would replace politics by moral judgement, and would be a perfect society in the curious sense that there would be no crime, greed, or poverty because people would have been perfectly socialized. Since it would be a moral perfection without effort, we could describe it indifferently either as the triumph or the extinction of morality. Such is one version of the paradox we are exploring.

We may call this influential project 'political moralism'. It can be seen working in a number of different areas, and we may illustrate the way it works by looking at the project that the nationally sovereign state should be replaced by the emerging international moral order. Sometimes internationalism is presented as a project to be supported; more commonly it appears as an analysis of the inevitable (and desirable) movement of affairs.

The first problem to which internationalism is an answer is that of war. We earlier saw that dynasties were thought to be the cause of war, and republics the solution. In this new version of the claim that war results from bad institutions, the nationally sovereign state is taken to be the cause of war, and the growth of international government to be the solution. The theory that bad institutions cause social evils assumes that human beings are plastic creatures who reflect the institutions in which they find themselves. It assumes, that is to say, that there is little or nothing that can be called 'human nature'. If human beings are malleable in this way, then it would seem to follow that we might be able to solve not merely the problem of war but the even more fundamental problem of justice itself. And, following this thought, some internationalists seek nothing less than a just distribution among all the peoples of the world of the material and moral benefits (namely, rights) available in the modern world. As this doctrine is spelled out, the ambition to replace politics by morality is revealed as involving abolishing the two central pillars of politics: the individual, as self-interested, and the nation-state, on the ground that it is merely the organization of collective selfishness, sometimes called nationalism. Morality in this form of argument is identified with nothing else but unselfish giving, and politics is taken to be a dirty business.

A project of this kind needs to explain why all the generations from Adam to Aquarius have failed to make much progress on this major improvement in the human condition, and here the argument of contemporary political moralism borrows an explanation from ideology. Justice has hitherto been blocked (so it is said) by the interests of the dominant élites who have always controlled the state. In older versions, this argument juxtaposed rich and poor, bourgeoisie and proletariat, imperialists and subject peoples. More recent theory has focused on the relationship of oppression: whites oppressing blacks, men oppressing women, and so on. And while much of this is melodramatic caricature, it does correspond to one central feature of politics from the days of Solon to the present.

That feature is the fact that politics has been the business of the powerful: citizens, nobles, property-owners, patriarchs – all had power and status. It was essential to the idea of the state, in all its forms, that it should be an association of *independent* disposers of their own resources. The rights of this élite were, over the centuries, generalized to become the modern rights of universal citizenship, but they first became operational as the status enjoyed by the powerful few. It was precisely because the state was composed of masterful characters that it could not turn into a despotism. Having projects of their own, powerful individuals of this kind had no inclination whatever to become the instruments of someone else's project. This is the sense in which despotism and politics are precisely opposed, and the state was distinguished by the right of the individual to dispose of his (and in time her) own property.

Political moralism, however, takes the independence of citizens not as a guarantee of freedom but as a barrier to the project of moralizing the world. Independent individuals disposing of their own property as they please are identified with selfishness and taken to be the cause of poverty. A socially just world is thought to require a rational distribution of the goods which pour so abundantly forth in a modern society. But states whose authority is constitutionally limited to ruling by law are imperfect instruments for the immense task of rational distribution, and of the resulting necessity of rectifying the attitudes on which injustice is founded. The entity called 'the state' could, however, become adequate to this formidable task if it were to change its character. And this character does in fact tend to change with every access of central power to dispose of the wealth an economy generates.

Modern politics is thus generating a remarkable dilemma. Moralizing the human condition is only possible if we can make the world correspond to some conception of social justice. But it turns out that we can only transcend the inequalities of the past if we institute precisely the form of social order – a despotism – which Western civilization has immemorially found incompatible with its free and independent customs. The promise is justice, the price is freedom.

Like everything else in life, politics is about hard choices, and the nicest thing to do with a hard choice is to evade it. Semantic abracadabra helps. A quite new sense of 'politics' has emerged to do this work, and unless we keep track of it we are all at sea in understanding the modern world. The essence of this new meaning is that 'politics' is made to cover every small detail of life. It is a semantic drift which happens quite unselfconsciously. Let me illustrate at random. The images of a photographer who has blown up the wrist scars from a suicide attempt are described in the press as 'a finely tuned balance between the confessional, the formal and the political'. The producer of a television soap opera who has put child-beating, lesbianism, kidnapping, and other social issues into the programme is quoted as saying: 'It's been my conscious decision to put politics back into the programme.' Here politics has broken out from its familiar haunts in legislatures, ministries, and hustings and roams the streets and invades the remotest corners of kitchen and bedroom. It has become identical with values as a whole.

Let us make the contrast precise: politics in the modern world has generally been the activity of dealing with the business of a civil association, the state, which provided the formal framework within which individuals could produce and consume, associate socially with each other, worship or not worship, and express themselves in art. Politics was strictly defined by its limits, and the limit was what was necessary for this complex civilization to work.

In this new sense of politics, however, there are no limits: where people cut their wrists, or children are beaten, or lesbians are not fully accepted, *political* action ought to be taken, and what it requires is that attitudes should be changed in order that, ultimately, harmony will prevail. Politics becomes, in a famous formula in political science, 'the authoritative allocation of values'. In other words, it is the business of society to tell us what we should admire and condemn.

It would be hard to exaggerate the range and significance of this transformation. How has it been achieved? By what leverage? The broad answer is that public judgement has not only come to denigrate what is independent as selfish, but to focus upon the sufferings of the dependent poor as a moral indictment of our social arrangements. From early modern times, the state had arranged through the Poor Law that parishes should be responsible for the indigent, but except as on occasion threatening disorder, the poor have not until recent times been politically significant. In the course of the nineteenth century, however, as the suffrage broadened, welfare came to be as interesting to rulers as war had always been. Foreign enemies, on the one hand, and the poor on the other, were interesting politically because they constituted a reason for exercising dazzling powers of government and administration. The poor became so interesting, indeed, that they could not be allowed to fade away, and whole new definitions of poverty, as relative to rising levels of average income, were constructed in order not only to keep the poor in being but actually to increase their numbers. Simultaneously, new classes of supposedly oppressed members of contemporary society began to use poverty leverage to extract benefits in redistributive states.

This is how the state in the twentieth century discovered dependence, which had previously occupied no more than a small patch in the sphere of morality. One moral virtue, charity, in a politicized form, expanded to take over politics. This was a significant development for many reasons. One of them is that dependence is a particularly interesting concept, since it reveals the direction of religious thought. The essence of Christianity is that we are all entirely dependent creatures of God. The atheists of the nineteenth century thought God merely a consolatory fantasy, but were no less insistent that man was a dependent creature. Here, however, the dependence was not on God but on society. In Marxist terms, for example, bourgeois individualists, as people suffering from the illusion that they are self-created, correspond to those who in Christian terms suffer from the sin of pride: they have put themselves, instead of God (or society) at the centre of the universe. In terms of this new religious tendency, self-interest is a sin because it proclaims the self to be independent of society. The ideal is that we should all altruistically contribute to society, and receive from it only the health, education, and other services which society provides equally to all.

Politics is, then, so inextricably bound up with our humanity that a transformation of the state affects religion, culture, morality, and much else. This is no less true when the transformation is happening so gradually that we fail to notice it. Changes here are, as always, masked by the current moral pieties of a society. But we may analyse some aspects of political moralism by distinguishing between the *substance* and the *style* of politics. The substance of political moralism is to be found in the detailed moral attitudes it inculcates: namely that the relief of suffering requires us to be managed by experts who require of us a more self-sacrificing attitude to life.

The style is theoretical rather than practical, abstract rather than concrete. Since the French Revolution, politics has commonly been discussed in terms of doctrine and ideology rather than in terms of what local problems require of the legal system. Even where, as in the liberal democratic West, politics has not completely given way to ideology, it has everywhere been subject to a restless concern with action to implement blueprints for betterment. Tom Paine, for example, thought that the rights of man offered a theory to guide legislators in creating a better society, but he did not think that his generation had the right to bind its successors. In our more confidently theoretical days, politicians understand themselves as engaged in the task of founding once and for all a more just society. Once built, it will not need to be changed.

Its building-blocks are necessarily the hearts of individuals. It rests upon conduct flowing from the right attitudes. And here again we encounter a feature of modern political transformation whose character can best be grasped in the caricature of totalitarianism. It will be remembered that totalitarian leaders flattered and cajoled the masses, declaring them the inspiration of all progress, while in fact taking no notice of them, killing them, and imposing on them the dead weight of ideology. Modern democracies exhibit a parallel development. The rulers are elected by citizens, but treat those citizens as if they were stupid. Indeed, the paradox is that an electorate so confidently treated as stupid by its rulers should yet have the authority to elect those rulers. A notable contradiction is emerging between the theory and the practice of democracy.

The evidence that this is the case is now unmistakable. The French government, for example, mounts a campaign telling the French people they must be more polite to foreigners. The American government has a Surgeon General who tells Americans what they should eat and drink. In all countries, governments dictate educational policy on the ground that parents, or at least many parents, do not have the skill of knowing what is best for their children. Legislation in many countries covers such things as the jokes subjects may tell. The German government legislates to force its subjects to believe in the Holocaust. The British government supplies helpful guidance on the practice of safe sex.

These emerging features of modern government give us the clue to the significance of the poor and the dependent. They are the lever by which governments accumulate power over everyone, dependent and independent alike. The working assumption of political moralism is that everyone is both dependent and stupid, which is the safest assumption to make given that a perfect world cannot allow error to creep in. Morals and manners are feeble props of a perfect society because human beings often behave in immoral and ill-mannered ways. But it is not merely conduct which has become part of this new form of politics. The very character of the people must be changed, especially that of the groups identified as oppressors. Men must cease to be 'macho', employers less 'grasping', heterosexuals must abandon any 'privileging' their ideas on romance or the family, whites must become more considerate to blacks, and so on. And according to the medical authorities in all Western countries, everyone must become less obese, suicidal, and addicted to alcohol.

We may sum this up by saying that the more the style of what used to be called politics becomes theorized, the more political problems come to be reinterpreted as managerial. Working out the least oppressive laws under which different and sometimes conflicting groups may live peaceably together is being replaced by manipulation and management of the attitudes different groups take towards each other, with the hope that this will ultimately bring harmony. In other words, in this new form of society, human beings are becoming the matter which is to be shaped according to the latest moral ideas.

The echo of the past always illuminates. *Cui bono?* the Romans used to ask. Who benefits? In an egalitarian world, everyone is equal, except perhaps the managers of equality. And certainly in the foreseeable future, there will be endless and not unprofitable work for those whose business it is to spell out in ever greater detail the rules of the game of life, and to adjudicate conflict, and to teach the benighted what thoughts a just society requires. Politics will have died, but everything will be politics.

This introduction ends, then, with an example of political theory, an argument likely to provoke disagreement, perhaps even a bit of outrage. And if it does do that, it will have succeeded in illustrating one more aspect of the many-sided thing we have been studying. Farewell.

Further Reading

First, the classics of political thought, which are remarkably readable (that is how they got to be classics) and constitute a reference language in which all students of politics discuss the subject. Machiavellian, Hobbesian, Marxian, etc. are key political terms. The books listed here are available in a variety of different editions.

Plato: *The Republic*
Aristotle: *Politics*
Machiavelli: *The Prince*
Hobbes: *Leviathan*
Locke: *Second Treatise of Government*
Rousseau: *The Social Contract*
Burke: *Reflections on the Revolution in France*
John Stuart Mill: *On Liberty*
Karl Marx and Frederick Engels: *The Communist Manifesto*
Alexis de Tocqueville: *Democracy in America*

There are many useful introductory books about political science, international relations, political economy, and related subjects. The following are some significant works, most of which have stood the test of time.

Gabriel Almond and Sidney Verba: *The Civic Culture Revisited* (Sage, 1989).

Walter Bagehot: *The English Constitution* (Fontana, 1988).

Brian Barry: *Political Argument* (Harvester Wheatsheaf, 1990).

Hedley Bull: *The Anarchical Society* (Macmillan 1977, 2/e 1995).

Bernard Crick: *In Defence of Politics* (Penguin, 1993).

Louis Hartz: *The Liberal Tradition in America* (Harcourt Brace, 1962)

F. A. Hayek: *The Road to Serfdom* (Routledge, 1991).

Christopher Hood: *The Art of the State: Culture, Rhetoric, and Public Management* (Oxford University Press, 1998).

Elie Kedourie: *Nationalism* (Blackwell, 1993).

Ferdinand Mount: *The British Constitution Now* (Mandarin, 1993).

Michael Oakeshott: *Rationalism in Politics* (Liberty Press, 1991).

Mancur Olson: *The Logic of Collective Action* (Harvard University Press, 1965).

Arlene Saxonhouse: *Women in the History of Political Thought* (Praeger, 1985).

Robert Skidelsky: *The Road from Serfdom* (Penguin, 1995).

R. H. Tawney: *Equality* (Volume I of Theories of the Mixed Economy, ed. David Reismann, Pickering and Chatto, 1994).

Sidney Verba and Norman Nie: *Participation in America* (University of Chicago Press, 1987).

Kenneth Waltz: *Man, The State and War* (Columbia University Press, 1965).

Index

Politics